THE DAILY READING BIBLE

Volume 15

LUKE 9-15   JONAH   2 TIMOTHY

The Daily Reading Bible (Volume 15)
© Matthias Media 2008

Matthias Media
(St Matthias Press Ltd ACN 067 558 365)
PO Box 225
Kingsford NSW 2032
Australia
Ph: (02) 9663 1478; Int. +61-2-9663-1478
Fax: (02) 9663 3265; Int. +61-2-9663-3265
Email: info@matthiasmedia.com.au
Internet: www.matthiasmedia.com.au

Matthias Media (USA)
Ph: 724 964 8152; Int. +1-724-964-8152
Fax: 724 964 8166; Int. +1-724-964-8166
Email: sales@matthiasmedia.com
Internet: www.matthiasmedia.com

ISBN 978 1 921441 10 3

Cover design and typesetting by Matthias Media.

CONTENTS

CONTENTS

INTRODUCTION

Reading our Bibles regularly is getting **harder.** That, at least, seems to be the common experience of many Christians. We could waste lots of ink speculating on the reasons for this: is it the frenetic pace of life these days? Is it spiritual laziness? Is it the impact of postmodernism on our culture and the lack of certainty when it comes to interpreting the written word?

But a better option than speculating on the reasons, we thought, was to provide a new resource for Christians to help them get back into a more regular habit of reflecting daily on God's word. So back in June 2001, we decided to start including a section called 'Bible Brief' in our monthly magazine, *The Briefing* (see www.matthiasmedia.com.au for more information about *The Briefing*). The 'Bible Brief' provided 20 short readings each month—acknowledging that there will be days we miss or days when we want to do something a bit different—with questions, thoughts to ponder, and suggestions to get started in prayer.

Now, several years later, we have a good collection of 'Bible Briefs', and it's time to offer them to a wider audience in a format that will, we hope, be even more convenient and useful.

This fifteenth volume contains 60 readings, all designed to be done in 15–20 minutes. These daily Bible readings are designed to help you feed regularly from God's word. They won't cover every issue in each passage, nor even every passage from each Bible book. In other words, *they are no substitute for the in-depth study of the Scriptures* that you may undertake personally, in small groups or through listening to sermons.

With the kind permission of our friends at Crossway Bibles, we've been able to make this a complete package to take with you—we've included the English Standard Version Bible text with each daily study. So you can take this one book with you and have everything you need—on the train, on the bus, or to the park at lunchtime—wherever and whenever you can get 20 minutes to yourself.

How to use these readings
- *With a penitent heart*, the true prerequisite for all Bible reading. Open with prayer (perhaps using the prayer suggested at the beginning of each set of studies).
- *With 15–20 minutes* of peace and quiet. If you can take longer, and want to read and pray further—great! But we have designed the readings to be done in a fairly short space of time.
- *With an accurate modern translation.* We recommend and have included the new ESV translation. The writers of the studies refer to this translation. Contact us for further details about the ESV or visit www.matthiasmedia.com.au/ESV

- *With a pen.* Even if you only jot down brief ideas, writing focuses the mind.
- *As a guide and help, not a straitjacket.* Feel free to dig further into the passage, to notice and ponder things that the questions don't point to.
- *As a launch-pad for prayer.* Use the prayer ideas at the end of each reading as a starting point for your daily prayer. Many of the points that will arise from the readings will be things you can pray for yourself, and also for others (family, friends, neighbours, etc.). Why not compile a list of people you want to pray for (you can write them in the blank space below), and use the prayer ideas from each reading to pray for the next person on your list?

This fifteenth volume includes:
- studies on Luke 9-15 (written by Cameron Munro, Senior Associate Pastor of Trinity Hills, Aldgate, a church plant of Holy Trinity Adelaide in Australia)
- studies on Jonah (written by Andrew Reid, Old Testament and Hermeneutics lecturer at Ridley College in Melbourne, Australia)
- studies on 2 Timothy (written by Nigel Gordon who works with City Bible Forum and St Matthew's Shenton Park in Perth, Australia).

Matthias Media
August 2008

Please note: the main section of Scripture for each study is reproduced before the questions. Other Scripture references are reproduced as footnotes at the bottom of the page, or, where the passages are too long to be included as footnotes, in the appendix.

PEOPLE TO PRAY FOR:

LUKE 9-15

INTRODUCTION

After Peter's declaration of Jesus' identity ("The Christ of God" in Luke 9:20), Jesus sets out for Jerusalem and the cross. Luke's Gospel shifts at this point and records Jesus' teaching about the need to respond to him in faithful discipleship. These readings focus on the first half of Jesus' journey to Jerusalem.

You might like to use this prayer (or your own variation of it) before each of the next 20 studies:

Dear Father,
Show me in your word the road I am to walk as I follow in the footsteps of your Son.
Challenge me and change me so that I will live for you every day. I ask this in Christ's name.
Amen

Notes: In this set of studies, you'll find various quotes ('What someone else said') in place of the usual 'Ponder' section. You might like to take a minute to reflect on the quote and how it summarizes the passage, deepens your understanding of the passage or spurs you on in your daily walk.

NB: Tick the box when you've completed each study ✓

| READING 1 | LUKE 9:51-62 | |

When the days drew near for [Jesus] to be taken up, he set his face to go to Jerusalem. ⁵² And he sent messengers ahead of him, who went and entered a village of the Samaritans, to make preparations for him. ⁵³ But the people did not receive him, because his face was set toward Jerusalem. ⁵⁴ And when his disciples James and John saw it, they said, "Lord, do you want us to tell fire to come down from heaven and consume them?" ⁵⁵ But he turned and rebuked them. ⁵⁶ And they went on to another village.

⁵⁷ As they were going along the road, someone said to him, "I will follow you wherever you go." ⁵⁸ And Jesus said to him, "Foxes have holes, and birds of the air have nests, but the Son of Man has nowhere to lay his head." ⁵⁹ To another he said, "Follow me." But he said, "Lord, let me first go and bury my father." ⁶⁰ And Jesus said to him, "Leave the dead to bury their own dead. But as for you, go and proclaim the kingdom of God." ⁶¹ Yet another said, "I will follow you, Lord, but let me first say farewell to those at my home." ⁶² Jesus said to him, "No one who puts his hand to the plow and looks back is fit for the kingdom of God."

1. What different responses to Jesus do you see here?

2. What things hold people back from committing to Jesus?

3. What right does Jesus have to expect such radical commitment?

4. If he spoke to you, what might he say is more important to you than him?

WHAT SOMEONE ELSE SAID

"Were the whole realm of nature mine,
That were an offering far too small,
Love so amazing so divine,
Demands my life, my soul, my all."
(Isaac Watts, in the hymn
'When I Survey the Wondrous Cross.'[1])

PRAYER IDEAS Ask God to give you an undivided heart that seeks to follow him before all things and does not sacrifice the best for the good.

READING 2   LUKE 10:1-16

After this the Lord appointed seventy-two others and sent them on ahead of him, two by two, into every town and place where he himself was about to go. 2 And he said to them, "The harvest is plentiful, but the laborers are few. Therefore pray earnestly to the Lord of the harvest to send out laborers into his harvest. 3 Go your way; behold, I am sending you out as lambs in the midst of wolves. 4 Carry no moneybag, no knapsack, no sandals, and greet no one on the road. 5 Whatever house you enter, first say, 'Peace be to this house!' 6 And if a son of peace is there, your peace will rest upon him. But if not, it will return to you. 7 And remain in the same house, eating and drinking what they provide, for the laborer deserves his wages. Do not go from house to house. 8 Whenever you enter a town and they receive you, eat what is set before you. 9 Heal the sick in it and say to them, 'The kingdom of God has come near to you.' 10 But whenever you enter a town and they do not receive you, go into its streets and say, 11 'Even the dust of your town that clings to our feet we wipe off against you. Nevertheless know this, that the kingdom of God has come near.' 12 I tell you, it will be more bearable on that day for Sodom than for that town.

13 "Woe to you, Chorazin! Woe to you, Bethsaida! For if the mighty works done in you had been done in Tyre and Sidon, they would have repented long ago, sitting in sackcloth and ashes. 14 But it will be more bearable in the judgement for Tyre and Sidon than for you. 15 And you, Capernaum, will you be exalted to heaven? You shall be brought down to Hades.

16 "The one who hears you hears me, and the one who rejects you rejects me, and the one who rejects me rejects him who sent me."

---

1. 1707.

1. What is the 'harvest' (v. 2)?

2. As "lambs in the midst of wolves", why can you be confident?

3. What is Jesus trying to teach his disciples when he sends them out without resources? What does this teach you?

4. Why do you think people would reject the message?

WHAT SOMEONE ELSE SAID

"And I heard the voice of the Lord saying, 'Whom shall I send, and who will go for us?' Then I said, 'Here am I! Send me.'" (Isaiah, in Isaiah 6:8.)

PRAYER IDEAS

Ask God to open your eyes to his harvest and provide you with all you need to work faithfully amongst it.

READING 3   LUKE 10:17-24

The seventy-two returned with joy, saying, "Lord, even the demons are subject to us in your name!" 18 And he said to them, "I saw Satan fall like lightning from heaven. 19 Behold, I have given you authority to tread on serpents and scorpions, and over all the power of the enemy, and nothing shall hurt you. 20 Nevertheless, do not rejoice in this, that the spirits are subject to you, but rejoice that your names are written in heaven."

21 In that same hour he rejoiced in the Holy Spirit and said, "I thank you, Father, Lord of heaven and earth, that you have hidden these things from the wise and understanding and revealed them to little children; yes, Father, for such was your gracious will. 22 All things have been handed over to me by my Father, and no one knows who the Son is except the Father, or who the Father is except the Son and anyone to whom the Son chooses to reveal him."

23 Then turning to the disciples he said privately, "Blessed are the eyes that see what you see! 24 For I tell you that many prophets and kings desired to see what you see, and did not see it, and to hear what you hear, and did not hear it."

1. What have "the seventy-two" seen?

2. Why have these things happened (cf. 10:9²)?

3. What does Jesus reveal to his disciples? What do they 'see'?

WHAT SOMEONE ELSE SAID

"God chose what is low and despised in the world, even things that are not, to bring to

---

2. "Heal the sick in it and say to them, 'The kingdom of God has come near to you.'"

nothing things that are, so that no human being might boast in the presence of God." (Paul, in 1 Corinthians 1:28-29.)

PRAYER IDEAS Thank God for opening your eyes and your ears so that through Jesus Christ you can know him truly.

READING 4   LUKE 10:25-37

And behold, a lawyer stood up to put him to the test, saying, "Teacher, what shall I do to inherit eternal life?" 26 He said to him, "What is written in the Law? How do you read it?" 27 And he answered, "You shall love the Lord your God with all your heart and with all your soul and with all your strength and with all your mind, and your neighbor as yourself." 28 And he said to him, "You have answered correctly; do this, and you will live."

29 But he, desiring to justify himself, said to Jesus, "And who is my neighbor?" 30 Jesus replied, "A man was going down from Jerusalem to Jericho, and he fell among robbers, who stripped him and beat him and departed, leaving him half dead. 31 Now by chance a priest was going down that road, and when he saw him he passed by on the other side. 32 So likewise a Levite, when he came to the place and saw him, passed by on the other side. 33 But a Samaritan, as he journeyed, came to where he was, and when he saw him, he had compassion. 34 He went to him and bound up his wounds, pouring on oil and wine. Then he set him on his own animal and brought him to an inn and took care of him. 35 And the next day he took out two denarii and gave them to the innkeeper, saying, 'Take care of him, and whatever more you spend, I will repay you when I come back.' 36 Which of these three, do you think, proved to be a neighbor to the man who fell among the robbers?" 37 He said, "The one who showed him mercy." And Jesus said to him, "You go, and do likewise."

1. The lawyer desired a good thing. What was wrong with his thinking?

2. As far as God is concerned, what love is real love?

3. How do you show God's love to your neighbours?

WHAT SOMEONE ELSE SAID
"If a brother or sister is poorly clothed and lacking in daily food, and one of you says to them, 'Go in peace, be warmed and filled,' without giving them the things needed for the body, what good is that? So also faith by itself, if it does not have works, is dead." (James, in James 2:15-17.)

PRAYER IDEAS Ask God to give you such love for him in your heart by his Spirit that it cannot help but overflow into love for your neighbours.

Now as they went on their way, Jesus entered a village. And a woman named Martha welcomed him into her house. [39] And she had a sister called Mary, who sat at the Lord's feet and listened to his teaching. [40] But Martha was distracted with much serving. And she went up to him and said, "Lord, do you not care that my sister has left me to serve alone? Tell her then to help me." [41] But the Lord answered her, "Martha, Martha, you are anxious and troubled about many things, [42] but one thing is necessary. Mary has chosen the good portion, which will not be taken away from her."

1. What was Mary's priority?

2. What was Martha's difficulty?

3. What keeps you from 'sitting at the Lord's feet'?

WHAT SOMEONE ELSE SAID

"Therefore do not be anxious, saying, 'What shall we eat?' or 'What shall we drink?' or 'What shall we wear?' For the Gentiles seek after all these things, and your heavenly Father knows that you need them all. But seek first the kingdom of God and his righteousness, and all these things will be added to you." (Jesus, in Matthew 6:31-33.)

PRAYER IDEAS Ask God to give you a heart that seeks him first in all situations.

Now Jesus was praying in a certain place, and when he finished, one of his disciples said to him, "Lord, teach us to pray, as John taught his disciples." [2] And he said to them, "When you pray, say:

"Father, hallowed be your name.
Your kingdom come.
[3] Give us each day our daily bread,
[4] and forgive us our sins,
    for we ourselves forgive everyone who is
      indebted to us.
And lead us not into temptation."

[5] And he said to them, "Which of you who has a friend will go to him at midnight and say to him, 'Friend, lend me three loaves, [6] for a friend of mine has arrived on a journey, and I have nothing to set before him'; [7] and he will answer from within, 'Do not bother me; the door is now shut, and my children are with me in bed. I cannot get up and give you anything'? [8] I tell you, though he will not get up and give him anything because he is his friend, yet because of his impudence he will rise and give him whatever he needs. [9] And I tell you, ask, and it will be given to you; seek, and you will find; knock, and it will be opened to you. [10] For everyone who asks receives, and the one who seeks finds, and to the one who knocks it will be opened. [11] What father among you, if his son asks for a fish, will instead of a fish give him a serpent; [12] or if he asks for an egg, will give him a scorpion?

LUKE 9-15

JONAH

2 TIMOTHY

[13] If you then, who are evil, know how to give good gifts to your children, how much more will the heavenly Father give the Holy Spirit to those who ask him!"

1. What are the priorities of Jesus' prayers?

2. Do you need to be 'impudent' to gain God's attention?

3. What does Jesus promise about God's

response to your prayers? What does this say about you when you don't/won't pray?

WHAT SOMEONE ELSE SAID
"Where is our delight in praying? Where is our sense that we are meeting with the living God, that we are doing business with God, that we are interceding with genuine unction before the throne of grace?" (DA Carson, in *A Call to Spiritual Reformation.*[3])

PRAYER IDEAS Ask God to help you to become someone who desires the things that he desires above all things.

READING 7   LUKE 11:14-26

Now he was casting out a demon that was mute. When the demon had gone out, the mute man spoke, and the people marveled. [15] But some of them said, "He casts out demons by Beelzebul, the prince of demons," [16] while others, to test him, kept seeking from him a sign from heaven. [17] But he, knowing their thoughts, said to them, "Every kingdom divided against itself is laid waste, and a divided household falls. [18] And if Satan also is divided against himself, how will his kingdom stand? For you say that I cast out demons by Beelzebul. [19] And if I cast out demons by Beelzebul, by whom do your sons cast them out? Therefore they will be your judges. [20] But if it is by the finger of God that I cast out demons, then the kingdom of God has come upon you. [21] When a strong man, fully armed, guards his own palace, his goods are safe; [22] but when one stronger than he attacks him and overcomes him, he takes away his armor in which he trusted and divides his spoil. [23] Whoever is not with me is against me, and whoever does not gather with me scatters.

[24] "When the unclean spirit has gone out of a person, it passes through waterless places seeking rest, and finding none it says, 'I will return to my house from which I came.' [25] And when it comes, it finds the house swept and put in order. [26] Then it goes and brings seven other spirits more evil than itself, and they enter and dwell there. And the last state of that person is worse than the first."

1. What accusation is made against Jesus?

2. What alternative explanation does Jesus give for what they are seeing?

---

3. Baker Books, Grand Rapids, 1992, p. 17.

3. What decision does this leave us with?

WHAT SOMEONE ELSE SAID

"He has delivered us from the domain of darkness and transferred us to the kingdom of his beloved Son ..." (Paul, in Colossians 1:13.)

PRAYER IDEAS Thank God that Jesus has plundered the 'strong man's' kingdom and established you in the kingdom of God.

READING 8 — LUKE 11:27-36

As he said these things, a woman in the crowd raised her voice and said to him, "Blessed is the womb that bore you, and the breasts at which you nursed!" 28 But he said, "Blessed rather are those who hear the word of God and keep it!"

29 When the crowds were increasing, he began to say, "This generation is an evil generation. It seeks for a sign, but no sign will be given to it except the sign of Jonah. 30 For as Jonah became a sign to the people of Nineveh, so will the Son of Man be to this generation. 31 The queen of the South will rise up at the judgement with the men of this generation and condemn them, for she came from the ends of the earth to hear the wisdom of Solomon, and behold, something greater than Solomon is here. 32 The men of Nineveh will rise up at the judgement with this generation and condemn it, for they repented at the preaching of Jonah, and behold, something greater than Jonah is here.

33 "No one after lighting a lamp puts it in a cellar or under a basket, but on a stand, so that those who enter may see the light. 34 Your eye is the lamp of your body. When your eye is healthy, your whole body is full of light, but when it is bad, your body is full of darkness. 35 Therefore be careful lest the light in you be darkness. 36 If then your whole body is full of light, having no part dark, it will be wholly bright, as when a lamp with its rays gives you light."

1. What attitude and response was Jesus attacking?

2. Why was this attitude and response lacking?

3. What did Jesus expect people to do in response to him?

4. Do you see evidence of the people's attitude and response in your life? How do you respond to Christ?

WHAT SOMEONE ELSE SAID

"The church is nothing other than the movement launched into the public life of the world by its sovereign Lord to continue that which he came to do until it is finished in his return in glory." (Lesslie Newbigin, in *The Gospel in a Pluralist Society.*[4])

---

4. Eerdmans, Grand Rapids, 1989, p. 221.

Ask God to grant you true repentance and to help you to shape your life by his Spirit so that you will shine as a light in this dark world.

READING 9   LUKE 11:37-54

While Jesus was speaking, a Pharisee asked him to dine with him, so he went in and reclined at table. 38 The Pharisee was astonished to see that he did not first wash before dinner. 39 And the Lord said to him, "Now you Pharisees cleanse the outside of the cup and of the dish, but inside you are full of greed and wickedness. 40 You fools! Did not he who made the outside make the inside also? 41 But give as alms those things that are within, and behold, everything is clean for you.

42 "But woe to you Pharisees! For you tithe mint and rue and every herb, and neglect justice and the love of God. These you ought to have done, without neglecting the others. 43 Woe to you Pharisees! For you love the best seat in the synagogues and greetings in the marketplaces. 44 Woe to you! For you are like unmarked graves, and people walk over them without knowing it."

45 One of the lawyers answered him, "Teacher, in saying these things you insult us also." 46 And he said, "Woe to you lawyers also! For you load people with burdens hard to bear, and you yourselves do not touch the burdens with one of your fingers. 47 Woe to you! For you build the tombs of the prophets whom your fathers killed. 48 So you are witnesses and you consent to the deeds of your fathers, for they killed them, and you build their tombs. 49 Therefore also the Wisdom of God said, 'I will send them prophets and apostles, some of whom they will kill and persecute,' 50 so that the blood of all the prophets, shed from the foundation of the world, may be charged against this generation, 51 from the blood of Abel to the blood of Zechariah, who perished between the altar and the sanctuary. Yes, I tell you, it will be required of this generation. 52 Woe to you lawyers! For you have taken away the key of knowledge. You did not enter yourselves, and you hindered those who were entering."

53 As he went away from there, the scribes and the Pharisees began to press him hard and to provoke him to speak about many things, 54 lying in wait for him, to catch him in something he might say.

1. What is the heart of the Pharisee's problem?

2. What is the heart of the lawyer's problem?

3. How should they have responded?

4. How does your life measure up?

WHAT SOMEONE ELSE SAID

"Discipleship without Jesus Christ is ... devoid of all promise. Jesus will certainly reject it." (Dietrich Bonhoeffer, in *The Cost of Discipleship*.[5])

PRAYER IDEAS Ask God to so transform you by his grace that your life is lived out of a true response to God's love for you in Christ.

5. SCM, London, 2001, p. 17.

In the meantime, when so many thousands of the people had gathered together that they were trampling one another, he began to say to his disciples first, "Beware of the leaven of the Pharisees, which is hypocrisy. [2] Nothing is covered up that will not be revealed, or hidden that will not be known. [3] Therefore whatever you have said in the dark shall be heard in the light, and what you have whispered in private rooms shall be proclaimed on the housetops.

[4] "I tell you, my friends, do not fear those who kill the body, and after that have nothing more that they can do. [5] But I will warn you whom to fear: fear him who, after he has killed, has authority to cast into hell. Yes, I tell you, fear him! [6] Are not five sparrows sold for two pennies? And not one of them is forgotten before God. [7] Why, even the hairs of your head are all numbered. Fear not; you are of more value than many sparrows.

[8] "And I tell you, everyone who acknowledges me before men, the Son of Man also will acknowledge before the angels of God, [9] but the one who denies me before men will be denied before the angels of God. [10] And everyone who speaks a word against the Son of Man will be forgiven, but the one who blasphemes against the Holy Spirit will not be forgiven. [11] And when they bring you before the synagogues and the rulers and the authorities, do not be anxious about how you should defend yourself or what you should say, [12] for the Holy Spirit will teach you in that very hour what you ought to say."

1. Who or what do you fear?

2. How should the fear of God change your daily life?

3. What comfort is offered to those who fear God?

WHAT SOMEONE ELSE SAID
"Faint not nor fear, his arms are near,
He changes not and you are dear,
Only believe and you shall see,
That Christ is all in all to thee."
(John Monsell, in the hymn 'Fight the Good Fight'.[6])

PRAYER IDEAS Ask God to give you the strength to stand for him and confess his name.

Someone in the crowd said to him, "Teacher, tell my brother to divide the inheritance with me." [14] But he said to him, "Man, who made me a judge or arbitrator over you?" [15] And he said to them, "Take care, and be on your guard against all covetousness, for one's life does not consist in the abundance of his possessions." [16] And he told them a parable, saying, "The land of a rich man produced plentifully, [17] and he

6. 1863.

LUKE 9-15

JONAH

2 TIMOTHY

thought to himself, 'What shall I do, for I have nowhere to store my crops?' [18] And he said, 'I will do this: I will tear down my barns and build larger ones, and there I will store all my grain and my goods. [19] And I will say to my soul, Soul, you have ample goods laid up for many years; relax, eat, drink, be merry.' [20] But God said to him, 'Fool! This night your soul is required of you, and the things you have prepared, whose will they be?' [21] So is the one who lays up treasure for himself and is not rich toward God."

1. Was it wrong for this man to seek a share of the inheritance? Why or why not?

2. How do you see the 'rich man' in your society? What does he look like? What does he do?

3. How do you become rich toward God?

WHAT SOMEONE ELSE SAID
"The root of all evil is that we are the kind of people who settle for the love of money instead of the love of God." (John Piper, in *Desiring God.*[7])

PRAYER IDEAS Think about your attitude towards money and possessions, and ask God to help you to be rich toward him.

READING 12   LUKE 12:22-34

And he said to his disciples, "Therefore I tell you, do not be anxious about your life, what you will eat, nor about your body, what you will put on. [23] For life is more than food, and the body more than clothing. [24] Consider the ravens: they neither sow nor reap, they have neither storehouse nor barn, and yet God feeds them. Of how much more value are you than the birds! [25] And which of you by being anxious can add a single hour to his span of life? [26] If then you are not able to do as small a thing as that, why are you anxious about the rest? [27] Consider the lilies, how they grow: they neither toil nor spin, yet I tell you, even Solomon in all his glory was not arrayed like one of these. [28] But if God so clothes the grass, which is alive in the field today, and tomorrow is thrown into the oven, how much more will he clothe you, O you of little faith! [29] And do not seek what you are to eat and what you are to drink, nor be worried. [30] For all the nations of the world seek after these things, and your Father knows that you need them. [31] Instead, seek his kingdom, and these things will be added to you.

[32] "Fear not, little flock, for it is your Father's good pleasure to give you the kingdom. [33] Sell your possessions, and give to the needy. Provide yourselves with moneybags that do not grow old, with a treasure in the heavens that does not fail, where no thief approaches and no moth destroys. [34] For where your treasure is, there will your heart be also."

7. 3rd edn, Multnomah, Sisters, 2003 (1986), p. 186.

1. It is claimed that our society lives in a state of anxiety. What are you worried about? Make a list.

4. What does your security depend upon?

2. What is Jesus' remedy?

WHAT SOMEONE ELSE SAID

"[D]o not be anxious about anything, but in everything by prayer and supplication with thanksgiving let your requests be made known to God. And the peace of God, which surpasses all understanding, will guard your hearts and your minds in Christ Jesus." (Paul, in Philippians 4:6-7.)

3. Why do you need to hear Jesus' words to you?

PRAYER IDEAS Bring your list of worries before God in prayer. Ask him to guard your heart and mind in Christ Jesus.

READING 13   LUKE 12:35-53

"Stay dressed for action and keep your lamps burning, 36 and be like men who are waiting for their master to come home from the wedding feast, so that they may open the door to him at once when he comes and knocks. 37 Blessed are those servants whom the master finds awake when he comes. Truly, I say to you, he will dress himself for service and have them recline at table, and he will come and serve them. 38 If he comes in the second watch, or in the third, and finds them awake, blessed are those servants! 39 But know this, that if the master of the house had known at what hour the thief was coming, he would not have left his house to be broken into. 40 You also must be ready, for the Son of Man is coming at an hour you do not expect."

41 Peter said, "Lord, are you telling this parable for us or for all?" 42 And the Lord said, "Who then is the faithful and wise manager, whom his master will set over his household, to give them their portion of food at the proper time? 43 Blessed is that servant whom his master will find so doing when he comes. 44 Truly, I say to you, he will set him over all his possessions. 45 But if that servant says to himself, 'My master is delayed in coming,' and begins to beat the male and female servants, and to eat and drink and get drunk, 46 the master of that servant will come on a day when he does not expect him and at an hour he does not know, and will cut him in pieces and put him with the unfaithful. 47 And that servant who knew his master's will but did not get ready or act according to his will, will receive a severe beating. 48 But the one who did not know, and did what deserved a beating, will receive a light beating. Everyone to whom much was given, of him much will be required, and from him to whom they entrusted much, they will demand the more.

49 "I came to cast fire on the earth, and would that it were already kindled! 50 I have a baptism to be baptized with, and how great is my distress until it is accomplished! 51 Do you think that I have come to give peace on

earth? No, I tell you, but rather division. 52 For from now on in one house there will be five divided, three against two and two against three. 53 They will be divided, father against son and son against father, mother against daughter and daughter against mother, mother-in-law against her daughter-in-law and daughter-in-law against mother-in-law."

1. Why must you be alert?

2. What does it mean for us to 'stay alert'? What must you do while you wait?

3. What radical thing does Jesus promise if you do? What is the danger for the one who is not ready?

WHAT SOMEONE ELSE SAID

"Our whole work must be carried on under a deep sense of our own insufficiency, and our entire dependence upon Christ. We must go for light, and life, and strength to him who sends us on the work." (Richard Baxter, in *The Reformed Pastor.*[8])

PRAYER IDEAS Ask God for the endurance to live faithfully for him as you await his return.

READING 14 · LUKE 12:54-13:9

He also said to the crowds, "When you see a cloud rising in the west, you say at once, 'A shower is coming.' And so it happens. 55 And when you see the south wind blowing, you say, 'There will be scorching heat,' and it happens. 56 You hypocrites! You know how to interpret the appearance of earth and sky, but why do you not know how to interpret the present time?

57 "And why do you not judge for yourselves what is right? 58 As you go with your accuser before the magistrate, make an effort to settle with him on the way, lest he drag you to the judge, and the judge hand you over to the officer, and the officer put you in prison. 59 I tell you, you will never get out until you have paid the very last penny."

13:1 There were some present at that very time who told him about the Galileans whose blood Pilate had mingled with their sacrifices. 2 And he answered them, "Do you think that these Galileans were worse sinners than all the other Galileans, because they suffered in this way? 3 No, I tell you; but unless you repent, you will all likewise perish. 4 Or those eighteen on whom the tower in Siloam fell and killed them: do you think that they were worse offenders than all the others who lived in Jerusalem? 5 No, I tell you; but unless you repent, you will all likewise perish."

6 And he told this parable: "A man had a fig tree planted in his vineyard, and he came seeking fruit on it and found none. 7 And he said to the vinedresser, 'Look, for three years now I have come seeking fruit on this fig tree, and I find none. Cut it down. Why should it use up the ground?' 8 And he answered him, 'Sir, let it alone this year also, until I dig around it and put on manure. 9 Then if it should bear fruit next year, well and good; but if not, you can cut it down.'"

---

8. Banner of Truth, Edinburgh, 1974, p. 122.

Jesus begins this speech with a warning about the 'time'. He challenges his hearers with the fact that his presence means judgement.

1. *What warnings does Jesus give in this passage?*

2. *How does the fact of God's judgement affect your daily life?*

WHAT SOMEONE ELSE SAID
"There is no greater backdrop to ... the good news of Christ, nothing that throws it more clearly into light and joy and fullness than the fact of judgement." (Bruce Milne, in *Preaching the Living Word.*[9])

PRAYER IDEAS Pray that God would again convict you about the reality of judgement and the wonder of grace.

POINTER vv. 6-9: The fig tree is a symbol for Israel.

READING 15 — LUKE 13:10-21

Now he was teaching in one of the synagogues on the Sabbath. [11] And there was a woman who had had a disabling spirit for eighteen years. She was bent over and could not fully straighten herself. [12] When Jesus saw her, he called her over and said to her, "Woman, you are freed from your disability." [13] And he laid his hands on her, and immediately she was made straight, and she glorified God. [14] But the ruler of the synagogue, indignant because Jesus had healed on the Sabbath, said to the people, "There are six days in which work ought to be done. Come on those days and be healed, and not on the Sabbath day." [15] Then the Lord answered him, "You hypocrites! Does not each of you on the Sabbath untie his ox or his donkey from the manger and lead it away to water it? [16] And ought not this woman, a daughter of Abraham whom Satan bound for eighteen years, be loosed from this bond on the Sabbath day?" [17] As he said these things, all his adversaries were put to shame, and all the people rejoiced at all the glorious things that were done by him.

[18] He said therefore, "What is the kingdom of God like? And to what shall I compare it? [19] It is like a grain of mustard seed that a man took and sowed in his garden, and it grew and became a tree, and the birds of the air made nests in its branches."

[20] And again he said, "To what shall I compare the kingdom of God? [21] It is like leaven that a woman took and hid in three measures of flour, until it was all leavened."

The power that Jesus displays in the healing of the crippled woman is the small beginning of the kingdom of God breaking in.

1. *What is the promise that Jesus makes in the parable about the kingdom?*

2. *What makes you doubt the truth of Jesus' promise?*

---

9. David Jackman (ed.), Christian Focus Publications, Fearn, 1999, p. 78.

WHAT SOMEONE ELSE SAID

"[O]n this rock I will build my church, and the gates of hell shall not prevail against it." (Jesus, in Matthew 16:18.)

PRAYER IDEAS Ask God to give you eyes to see the growth of his kingdom.

READING 16 — LUKE 13:22-30

He went on his way through towns and villages, teaching and journeying toward Jerusalem. 23 And someone said to him, "Lord, will those who are saved be few?" And he said to them, 24 "Strive to enter through the narrow door. For many, I tell you, will seek to enter and will not be able. 25 When once the master of the house has risen and shut the door, and you begin to stand outside and to knock at the door, saying, 'Lord, open to us,' then he will answer you, 'I do not know where you come from.' 26 Then you will begin to say, 'We ate and drank in your presence, and you taught in our streets.' 27 But he will say, 'I tell you, I do not know where you come from. Depart from me, all you workers of evil!' 28 In that place there will be weeping and gnashing of teeth, when you see Abraham and Isaac and Jacob and all the prophets in the kingdom of God but you yourselves cast out. 29 And people will come from east and west, and from north and south, and recline at table in the kingdom of God. 30 And behold, some are last who will be first, and some are first who will be last."

1. *Who is the master of the house?*

2. *Who is the house open to? What determines whether they come in?*

3. *Are you known to the master of the house? How do you know?*

WHAT SOMEONE ELSE SAID

"And there is salvation in no one else, for there is no other name under heaven given among men by which we must be saved." (Peter, in Acts 4:12.)

PRAYER IDEAS Ask God to help you to see that 'knowing the master' is the best thing in life.

READING 17 — LUKE 13:31-14:6

At that very hour some Pharisees came and said to him, "Get away from here, for Herod wants to kill you." 32 And he said to them, "Go and tell that fox, 'Behold, I cast out demons and perform cures today and tomorrow, and the third day I finish my course. 33 Nevertheless, I must go on my way today and tomorrow and the day following, for it cannot be that a prophet should perish away from Jerusalem.' 34 O Jerusalem, Jerusalem, the city that kills the prophets and stones those who are sent to it! How often would I have gathered your children together as a hen gathers her brood under her wings, and you would not! 35 Behold, your house is forsaken. And I tell you, you will not see me until you say, 'Blessed is he who comes in the name of the Lord!'"

14:1 One Sabbath, when he went to dine at the house of a ruler of the Pharisees, they were watching him carefully. ² And behold, there was a man before him who had dropsy. ³ And Jesus responded to the lawyers and Pharisees, saying, "Is it lawful to heal on the Sabbath, or not?" ⁴ But they remained silent. Then he took him and healed him and sent him away. ⁵ And he said to them, "Which of you, having a son or an ox that has fallen into a well on a Sabbath day, will not immediately pull him out?" ⁶ And they could not reply to these things.

1. What is Jesus' attitude towards Jerusalem?

2. What attitude does Jerusalem have towards him? Where do you see this attitude in the Pharisees?

3. How does Jesus' attitude challenge your own?

WHAT SOMEONE ELSE SAID
"For I could wish that I myself were accursed and cut off from Christ for the sake of my brothers, my kinsmen according to the flesh." (Paul, in Romans 9:3.)

PRAYER IDEAS Ask God to have mercy on the Jewish people and gather them to himself.

READING 18   LUKE 14:7-24

Now he told a parable to those who were invited, when he noticed how they chose the places of honor, saying to them, ⁸ "When you are invited by someone to a wedding feast, do not sit down in a place of honor, lest someone more distinguished than you be invited by him, ⁹ and he who invited you both will come and say to you, 'Give your place to this person,' and then you will begin with shame to take the lowest place. ¹⁰ But when you are invited, go and sit in the lowest place, so that when your host comes he may say to you, 'Friend, move up higher.' Then you will be honored in the presence of all who sit at table with you. ¹¹ For everyone who exalts himself will be humbled, and he who humbles himself will be exalted."

¹² He said also to the man who had invited him, "When you give a dinner or a banquet, do not invite your friends or your brothers or your relatives or rich neighbors, lest they also invite you in return and you be repaid. ¹³ But when you give a feast, invite the poor, the crippled, the lame, the blind, ¹⁴ and you will be blessed, because they cannot repay you. For you will be repaid at the resurrection of the just."

¹⁵ When one of those who reclined at table with him heard these things, he said to him, "Blessed is everyone who will eat bread in the kingdom of God!" ¹⁶ But he said to him, "A man once gave a great banquet and invited many. ¹⁷ And at the time for the banquet he sent his servant to say to those who had been invited, 'Come, for everything is now ready.' ¹⁸ But they all alike began to make excuses. The first said to him, 'I have bought a field, and I must go out and see it. Please have me excused.' ¹⁹ And another said, 'I have bought five yoke of oxen, and I go to examine them. Please have me excused.' ²⁰ And another said, 'I have married a wife, and therefore

I cannot come.' ²¹ So the servant came and reported these things to his master. Then the master of the house became angry and said to his servant, 'Go out quickly to the streets and lanes of the city, and bring in the poor and crippled and blind and lame.' ²² And the servant said, 'Sir, what you commanded has been done, and still there is room.' ²³ And the master said to the servant, 'Go out to the highways and hedges and compel people to come in, that my house may be filled. ²⁴ For I tell you, none of those men who were invited shall taste my banquet.'"

1. When are you tempted to put yourself forward?

2. In the end, in whose eyes is it important to be significant?

3. Understanding that verses 16-24 are spoken as a warning against the Jewish people, where are the Gentiles in the parable?

4. What is your response to Jesus' words?

WHAT SOMEONE ELSE SAID

"After this I looked, and behold, a great multitude that no one could number, from every nation, from all tribes and peoples and languages, standing before the throne and before the Lamb, clothed in white robes, with palm branches in their hands ..." (John, in Revelation 7:9.)

PRAYER IDEAS Praise God for his wonderful plan to make one new people in Christ.

READING 19   LUKE 14:25-35

Now great crowds accompanied him, and he turned and said to them, ²⁶ "If anyone comes to me and does not hate his own father and mother and wife and children and brothers and sisters, yes, and even his own life, he cannot be my disciple. ²⁷ Whoever does not bear his own cross and come after me cannot be my disciple. ²⁸ For which of you, desiring to build a tower, does not first sit down and count the cost, whether he has enough to complete it? ²⁹ Otherwise, when he has laid a foundation and is not able to finish, all who see it begin to mock him, ³⁰ saying, 'This man began to build and was not able to finish.' ³¹ Or what king, going out to encounter another king in war, will not sit down first and deliberate whether he is able with ten thousand to meet him who comes against him with twenty thousand? ³² And if not, while the other is yet a great way off, he sends a delegation and asks for terms of peace. ³³ So therefore, any one of you who does not renounce all that he has cannot be my disciple.

³⁴ "Salt is good, but if salt has lost its taste, how shall its saltiness be restored? ³⁵ It is of no use either for the soil or for the manure pile. It is thrown away. He who has ears to hear, let him hear."

Jesus is making a point by exaggeration—that is, he is to be number one.

1. Where in your life do you need to 'hate' your family and self?

2. Can you afford to accept Jesus' call (vv. 28-30)?

3. Can you afford <u>not</u> to accept Jesus' call (vv. 31-33)?

WHAT SOMEONE ELSE SAID
"My utmost for his highest." (Oswald Chambers, in *My Utmost for His Highest*.[10])

PRAYER IDEAS Ask God to give you all you need to put him first in all things.

READING 20   LUKE 15:1-32

Now the tax collectors and sinners were all drawing near to hear him. [2] And the Pharisees and the scribes grumbled, saying, "This man receives sinners and eats with them."

[3] So he told them this parable: [4] "What man of you, having a hundred sheep, if he has lost one of them, does not leave the ninety-nine in the open country, and go after the one that is lost, until he finds it? [5] And when he has found it, he lays it on his shoulders, rejoicing. [6] And when he comes home, he calls together his friends and his neighbors, saying to them, 'Rejoice with me, for I have found my sheep that was lost.' [7] Just so, I tell you, there will be more joy in heaven over one sinner who repents than over ninety-nine righteous persons who need no repentance.

[8] "Or what woman, having ten silver coins, if she loses one coin, does not light a lamp and sweep the house and seek diligently until she finds it? [9] And when she has found it, she calls together her friends and neighbors, saying, 'Rejoice with me, for I have found the coin that I had lost.' [10] Just so, I tell you, there is joy before the angels of God over one sinner who repents."

[11] And he said, "There was a man who had two sons. [12] And the younger of them said to his father, 'Father, give me the share of property that is coming to me.' And he divided his property between them. [13] Not many days later, the younger son gathered all he had and took a journey into a far country, and there he squandered his property in reckless living. [14] And when he had spent everything, a severe famine arose in that country, and he began to be in need. [15] So he went and hired himself out to one of the citizens of that country, who sent him into his fields to feed pigs. [16] And he was longing to be fed with the pods that the pigs ate, and no one gave him anything.

[17] "But when he came to himself, he said, 'How many of my father's hired servants have more than enough bread, but I perish here with hunger! [18] I will arise and go to my father, and I will say to him, "Father, I have sinned against heaven and before you. [19] I am no longer worthy to be called your son. Treat me as one of your hired servants."' [20] And he arose and came to his father. But while he was still a long way off, his father saw him and felt compassion, and ran and embraced him and kissed him. [21] And the son said to him, 'Father, I have sinned against heaven

---

10. Discovery House Publishers, Grand Rapids, 1963.

and before you. I am no longer worthy to be called your son.' 22 But the father said to his servants, 'Bring quickly the best robe, and put it on him, and put a ring on his hand, and shoes on his feet. 23 And bring the fattened calf and kill it, and let us eat and celebrate. 24 For this my son was dead, and is alive again; he was lost, and is found.' And they began to celebrate.

25 "Now his older son was in the field, and as he came and drew near to the house, he heard music and dancing. 26 And he called one of the servants and asked what these things meant. 27 And he said to him, 'Your brother has come, and your father has killed the fattened calf, because he has received him back safe and sound.' 28 But he was angry and refused to go in. His father came out and entreated him, 29 but he answered his father, 'Look, these many years I have served you, and I never disobeyed your command, yet you never gave me a young goat, that I might celebrate with my friends. 30 But when this son of yours came, who has devoured your property with prostitutes, you killed the fattened calf for him!' 31 And he said to him, 'Son, you are always with me, and all that is mine is yours. 32 It was fitting to celebrate and be glad, for this your brother was dead, and is alive; he was lost, and is found.'"

In this chapter, we see the Father's loving and compansionate nature—that is, his heart.

1. What makes him joyful (vv. 7, 10, 31-32)?

2. Does he ever give up? Why/why not?

3. Do you deserve such perseverance? What is your response?

WHAT SOMEONE ELSE SAID
"O Love divine, what hast thou done!
The immortal God hath died for me!
The Father's co-eternal Son
Bore all my sins upon the tree.
Th'immortal God for me hath died:
My Lord, my Love, is crucified!"
(Charles Wesley, in the hymn 'O Love Divine.'")

PRAYER IDEAS Ask God to give you a heart like his—passionate to see the lost found.

---

11. 1742.

JONAH

INTRODUCTION

The book of Jonah records one of the Bible's most famous stories. Thrown overboard from a ship he had boarded in order to try to escape God, the Old Testament prophet Jonah is 'rescued' by a whale or giant fish before he is spat out on a beach. He journeys to Nineveh where he declares the judgement and mercy of God, and wrestles with his own tormented heart. In this set of studies, we look at this marvellous book in detail, and consider some relevant material from the wisdom literature and the Gospels. This book reveals the kindness of God to us, as well as searching the unfaithfulness and bitterness of our own hearts.

You might like to use this prayer (or your own variation of it) before each of the next 20 studies:

Heavenly Father,
Your thoughts are beyond my thoughts and your ways are not like my own, yet you have revealed yourself to me in your word. Lead me in your truth and teach me, for you are my saviour. In your mercy and steadfast love, do not remember my sins. Strengthen my faith and renew my heart, for I wait on you.
Amen.

READING 21   BACKGROUND TO JONAH ■

2 Kings 14:23–29

In the fifteenth year of Amaziah the son of Joash, king of Judah, Jeroboam the son of Joash, king of Israel, began to reign in Samaria, and he reigned forty-one years. 24 And he did what was evil in the sight of the LORD. He did not depart from all the sins of Jeroboam the son of Nebat, which he made Israel to sin. 25 He restored the border of Israel from Lebo-hamath as far as the Sea of the Arabah, according to the word of the LORD, the God of Israel, which he spoke by his servant Jonah the son of Amittai, the prophet, who was from Gath-hepher. 26 For the LORD saw that the affliction of Israel was very bitter, for there was none left, bond or free, and there was none to help Israel. 27 But the LORD had not said that he would blot out the name of Israel from under heaven, so he saved them by the hand of Jeroboam the son of Joash.

28 Now the rest of the acts of Jeroboam and all that he did, and his might, how he fought, and how he restored Damascus and Hamath to Judah in Israel, are they not written in the Book of the Chronicles of the Kings of Israel? 29 And Jeroboam slept with his fathers, the kings of Israel, and Zechariah his son reigned in his place.

Jonah 1:2

"Arise, go to Nineveh, that great city, and call out against it, for their evil has come up before me."

Jonah 3:1-3

Then the word of the LORD came to Jonah the second time, saying, ² "Arise, go to Nineveh, that great city, and call out against it the message that I tell you." ³ So Jonah arose and went to Nineveh, according to the word of the LORD. Now Nineveh was an exceedingly great city, three days' journey in breadth.

Jonah 4:11

"And should not I pity Nineveh, that great city, in which there are more than 120,000 persons who do not know their right hand from their left, and also much cattle?"

Jeremiah 10:9

Beaten silver is brought from Tarshish, and gold from Uphaz.
They are the work of the craftsman and of the hands of the goldsmith;
their clothing is violet and purple;
they are all the work of skilled men.

Isaiah 66:19

"... and I will set a sign among them. And from them I will send survivors to the nations, to Tarshish, Pul, and Lud, who draw the bow, to Tubal and Javan, to the coastlands far away, that have not heard my fame or seen my glory. And they shall declare my glory among the nations."

1 Kings 10:22

For the king had a fleet of ships of Tarshish at sea with the fleet of Hiram. Once every three years the fleet of ships of Tarshish used to come bringing gold, silver, ivory, apes, and peacocks.

1. Read 2 Kings 14:23-29. This passage probably refers to the same 'Jonah'. When and where was Jonah a prophet?

2. Read Jonah 1:2, 3:1-3 and 4:11. What do you find out about the city of Nineveh from the book of Jonah? Why would Jonah not have wanted to go to Nineveh?

3. Read Jeremiah 10:9, Isaiah 66:19 and 1 Kings 10:22. What sorts of things is the city of Tarshish noted for in the Bible?

PRAYER IDEAS Ask God to teach you much about himself and his purposes in Christ as you study the book of Jonah.

POINTER At this time, Nineveh was probably the capital city of the nation of Assyria, the dominant world power in Jonah's day.

READING 22   JONAH 1:1-3 ▮

Now the word of the LORD came to Jonah the son of Amittai, saying, ² "Arise, go to Nineveh, that great city, and call out against it, for their evil has come up before me." ³ But Jonah rose to flee to Tarshish from the presence of the LORD. He went down to Joppa and found a ship going to Tarshish. So he paid the fare and went on board, to go with them to Tarshish, away from the presence of the LORD.

1. Read Isaiah 6 (in the appendix, p. 65). This passage records Isaiah's response to God's call to speak his word. What is Isaiah's reaction? What does he do?

3. Why do you think Jonah might have acted the way he did? (Stay tuned; he tells us himself later on.)

2. In many ways, Isaiah's response is much like the standard response of God's prophets to their calling. Read Jonah 1:1-3. How is Jonah's reaction different to this standard?

PONDER Do you ever feel like acting like Jonah when you hear God's word? Why?

PRAYER IDEAS Ask God to help you to respond appropriately to his word—in humility and reverent fear (cf. Isa 66:2b[12]).

READING 23   JONAH 1:4-17 (THE MARINERS' RESPONSE)

But the LORD hurled a great wind upon the sea, and there was a mighty tempest on the sea, so that the ship threatened to break up. [5] Then the mariners were afraid, and each cried out to his god. And they hurled the cargo that was in the ship into the sea to lighten it for them. But Jonah had gone down into the inner part of the ship and had lain down and was fast asleep. [6] So the captain came and said to him, "What do you mean, you sleeper? Arise, call out to your god! Perhaps the god will give a thought to us, that we may not perish."

[7] And they said to one another, "Come, let us cast lots, that we may know on whose account this evil has come upon us." So they cast lots, and the lot fell on Jonah. [8] Then they said to him, "Tell us on whose account this evil has come upon us. What is your occupation? And where do you come from? What is your country? And of what people are you?" [9] And he said to them, "I am a Hebrew, and I fear the LORD, the God of heaven, who made the sea and the dry land." [10] Then the men were exceedingly afraid and said to him, "What is this that you have done!" For the men knew that he was fleeing from the presence of the LORD, because he had told them.

[11] Then they said to him, "What shall we do to you, that the sea may quiet down for us?" For the sea grew more and more tempestuous. [12] He said to them, "Pick me up and hurl me into the sea; then the sea will quiet down for you, for I know it is because of me that this great tempest has come upon you." [13] Nevertheless, the men rowed hard to get back to dry land, but they could not, for the sea grew more and more tempestuous against them. [14] Therefore they called out to the LORD, "O LORD, let us not perish for this man's life, and lay not on us innocent blood, for you, O LORD, have done as it pleased you." [15] So they picked up Jonah and hurled

12. But this is the one to whom I will look:
    he who is humble and contrite in spirit
    and trembles at my word.

him into the sea, and the sea ceased from its raging. ¹⁶ Then the men feared the Lᴏʀᴅ exceedingly, and they offered a sacrifice to the Lᴏʀᴅ and made vows.

¹⁷ And the Lᴏʀᴅ appointed a great fish to swallow up Jonah. And Jonah was in the belly of the fish three days and three nights.

1. How do the mariners react to the storm at sea?

2. How do they react to Jonah's words and actions?

3. How do they react to their gods and to God? Are the mariners just superstitious or is their reaction more profound than this?

PONDER Do you know people who are like the mariners in their thoughts about God and in their reactions to him? Are there ways you can help them respond to God rightly?

PRAYER IDEAS Pray for people you know who don't know God. Ask God to change their hearts so that they will worship him as the true and living God.

READING 24   JONAH 1:4-17 (JONAH'S RESPONSE)

But the Lᴏʀᴅ hurled a great wind upon the sea, and there was a mighty tempest on the sea, so that the ship threatened to break up. ⁵ Then the mariners were afraid, and each cried out to his god. And they hurled the cargo that was in the ship into the sea to lighten it for them. But Jonah had gone down into the inner part of the ship and had lain down and was fast asleep. ⁶ So the captain came and said to him, "What do you mean, you sleeper? Arise, call out to your god! Perhaps the god will give a thought to us, that we may not perish."

⁷ And they said to one another, "Come, let us cast lots, that we may know on whose account this evil has come upon us." So they cast lots, and the lot fell on Jonah. ⁸ Then they said to him, "Tell us on whose account this evil has come upon us. What is your occupation? And where do you come from? What is your country? And of what people are you?" ⁹ And he said to them, "I am a Hebrew, and I fear the Lᴏʀᴅ, the God of heaven, who made the sea and the dry land." ¹⁰ Then the

men were exceedingly afraid and said to him, "What is this that you have done!" For the men knew that he was fleeing from the presence of the Lᴏʀᴅ, because he had told them.

¹¹ Then they said to him, "What shall we do to you, that the sea may quiet down for us?" For the sea grew more and more tempestuous. ¹² He said to them, "Pick me up and hurl me into the sea; then the sea will quiet down for you, for I know it is because of me that this great tempest has come upon you." ¹³ Nevertheless, the men rowed hard to get back to dry land, but they could not, for the sea grew more and more tempestuous against them. ¹⁴ Therefore they called out to the Lᴏʀᴅ, "O Lᴏʀᴅ, let us not perish for this man's life, and lay not on us innocent blood, for you, O Lᴏʀᴅ, have done as it pleased you." ¹⁵ So they picked up Jonah and hurled him into the sea, and the sea ceased from its raging. ¹⁶ Then the men feared the Lᴏʀᴅ exceedingly, and they offered a sacrifice to the Lᴏʀᴅ and made vows.

¹⁷ And the Lᴏʀᴅ appointed a great fish to

swallow up Jonah. And Jonah was in the belly of the fish three days and three nights.

1. How does Jonah react to the storm at sea?

2. How does he react to the mariner's words and actions?

3. How does he react to God?

4. What do you learn about God from this passage?

PONDER How do you feel about Jonah's reaction to what happens? Do you identify with him?

PRAYER IDEAS Pray about your own conduct among 'God-fearing' people who are not Christians. Ask God to help you to be an example to them of how to respond to God rightly.

READING 25   JONAH 1:4-17 (PUTTING IT TOGETHER)

But the LORD hurled a great wind upon the sea, and there was a mighty tempest on the sea, so that the ship threatened to break up. 5 Then the mariners were afraid, and each cried out to his god. And they hurled the cargo that was in the ship into the sea to lighten it for them. But Jonah had gone down into the inner part of the ship and had lain down and was fast asleep. 6 So the captain came and said to him, "What do you mean, you sleeper? Arise, call out to your god! Perhaps the god will give a thought to us, that we may not perish."

7 And they said to one another, "Come, let us cast lots, that we may know on whose account this evil has come upon us." So they cast lots, and the lot fell on Jonah. 8 Then they said to him, "Tell us on whose account this evil has come upon us. What is your occupation? And where do you come from? What is your country? And of what people are you?" 9 And he said to them, "I am a Hebrew, and I fear the LORD, the God of heaven, who made the sea and the dry land." 10 Then the men were exceedingly afraid and said to him, "What is this that you have done!" For the men knew that he was fleeing from the presence of the LORD, because he had told them.

11 Then they said to him, "What shall we do to you, that the sea may quiet down for us?" For the sea grew more and more tempestuous. 12 He said to them, "Pick me up and hurl me into the sea; then the sea will quiet down for you, for I know it is because of me that this great tempest has come upon you." 13 Nevertheless, the men rowed hard to get back to dry land, but they could not, for the sea grew more and more tempestuous against them. 14 Therefore they called out to the LORD, "O LORD, let us not perish for this man's life, and lay not on us innocent blood, for you, O LORD, have done as it pleased you." 15 So they picked up Jonah and hurled him into the sea, and the sea ceased from its raging. 16 Then the men feared the LORD exceedingly, and they offered a sacrifice to the LORD and made vows.

17 And the LORD appointed a great fish to swallow up Jonah. And Jonah was in the belly of the fish three days and three nights.

1. *Find the four instances where words related to being afraid appear.*

2. *Who says that they fear God? Who acts as though they fear God?*

3. *Sum up what you've found out about Jonah and the mariners in this passage. Who comes out better in terms of the way they respond to God? What do you think God might be trying to teach you in this passage?*

PONDER If you were in Jonah's place, how do you think your behaviour would compare with that of the mariners? Read the pointer below. Are there any areas of your life where you need to repent of the gap between what you say about God and how you live?

PRAYER IDEAS Ask God for forgiveness for the times when you profess his name but refuse to obey him. Thank him for the grace he has shown towards sinners in Jesus.

POINTER It is clear that Jonah possessed the benefits of being God's person but lacked an appropriate response to his word. Having heard about Jesus, you have a much clearer and fuller understanding of God and his purposes. Therefore, you may be even more culpable in your disobedience.

READING 26   PSALM 104

Bless the LORD, O my soul!
O LORD my God, you are very great!
You are clothed with splendor and majesty,
    ² covering yourself with light as with a garment,
    stretching out the heavens like a tent.
³ He lays the beams of his chambers on the waters;
he makes the clouds his chariot;
    he rides on the wings of the wind;
⁴ he makes his messengers winds,
    his ministers a flaming fire.

⁵ He set the earth on its foundations,
    so that it should never be moved.
⁶ You covered it with the deep as with a garment;
    the waters stood above the mountains.
⁷ At your rebuke they fled;
    at the sound of your thunder they took to flight.

⁸ The mountains rose, the valleys sank down
    to the place that you appointed for them.
⁹ You set a boundary that they may not pass,
    so that they might not again cover the earth.

¹⁰ You make springs gush forth in the valleys;
    they flow between the hills;
¹¹ they give drink to every beast of the field;
    the wild donkeys quench their thirst.
¹² Beside them the birds of the heavens dwell;
    they sing among the branches.
¹³ From your lofty abode you water the mountains;
    the earth is satisfied with the fruit of your work.

¹⁴ You cause the grass to grow for the
    livestock
  and plants for man to cultivate,
that he may bring forth food from the earth
    ¹⁵ and wine to gladden the heart of
      man,
oil to make his face shine
  and bread to strengthen man's heart.

¹⁶ The trees of the Lord are watered
    abundantly,
  the cedars of Lebanon that he planted.
¹⁷ In them the birds build their nests;
  the stork has her home in the fir trees.
¹⁸ The high mountains are for the wild
    goats;
  the rocks are a refuge for the rock
    badgers.

¹⁹ He made the moon to mark the seasons;
  the sun knows its time for setting.
²⁰ You make darkness, and it is night,
  when all the beasts of the forest creep
    about.
²¹ The young lions roar for their prey,
  seeking their food from God.
²² When the sun rises, they steal away
  and lie down in their dens.
²³ Man goes out to his work
  and to his labor until the evening.

²⁴ O Lord, how manifold are your works!
  In wisdom have you made them all;
  the earth is full of your creatures.
²⁵ Here is the sea, great and wide,
  which teems with creatures
      innumerable,
  living things both small and great.
²⁶ There go the ships,
  and Leviathan, which you formed to
    play in it.

²⁷ These all look to you,
  to give them their food in due season.

²⁸ When you give it to them, they gather
    it up;
  when you open your hand, they are
    filled with good things.
²⁹ When you hide your face, they are
    dismayed;
  when you take away their breath, they
    die
  and return to their dust.
³⁰ When you send forth your Spirit, they are
    created,
  and you renew the face of the ground.

³¹ May the glory of the Lord endure forever;
  may the Lord rejoice in his works,
³² who looks on the earth and it trembles,
  who touches the mountains and they
    smoke!
³³ I will sing to the Lord as long as I live;
  I will sing praise to my God while I have
    being.
³⁴ May my meditation be pleasing to him,
  for I rejoice in the Lord.
³⁵ Let sinners be consumed from the earth,
  and let the wicked be no more!
Bless the Lord, O my soul!
Praise the Lord!

*What great works of God are celebrated in
this psalm (cf. Jonah 1:9[13])?*

PONDER When was the last time you
pondered and celebrated God's great
creative work in making and sustaining the
world? What aspects of his creation are you
particularly grateful for?

PRAYER IDEAS Thank God for his creation of
and his sustaining of the world.

---

13. And he said to them, "I am a Hebrew, and I fear the Lord, the God of heaven, who made the sea and the dry land."

And the Lᴏʀᴅ appointed a great fish to swallow up Jonah. And Jonah was in the belly of the fish three days and three nights. **2:1** Then Jonah prayed to the Lᴏʀᴅ his God from the belly of the fish, ² saying,

"I called out to the Lᴏʀᴅ, out of my distress,
    and he answered me;
out of the belly of Sheol I cried,
    and you heard my voice.
³ For you cast me into the deep,
    into the heart of the seas,
    and the flood surrounded me;
all your waves and your billows
    passed over me.
⁴ Then I said, 'I am driven away
    from your sight;
yet I shall again look
    upon your holy temple.'
⁵ The waters closed in over me to take my
      life;
    the deep surrounded me;
weeds were wrapped about my head
      ⁶ at the roots of the mountains.
I went down to the land
    whose bars closed upon me forever;
yet you brought up my life from the pit,
    O Lᴏʀᴅ my God.
⁷ When my life was fainting away,
    I remembered the Lᴏʀᴅ,
and my prayer came to you,
    into your holy temple.
⁸ Those who pay regard to vain idols
    forsake their hope of steadfast love.
⁹ But I with the voice of thanksgiving
will sacrifice to you;
    what I have vowed I will pay.
      Salvation belongs to the Lᴏʀᴅ!"

¹⁰ And the Lᴏʀᴅ spoke to the fish, and it vomited Jonah out upon the dry land.

1. Jonah 1:15¹⁴ says that the mariners were responsible for hurling Jonah into the sea. Who does Jonah say was responsible? (Remember Psalm 104 from Reading 26.)

2. How is Jonah's response to God in this passage different to chapter 1? (Look over Readings 22 and 24.) Which parts of his prayer indicate the state of his heart?

PONDER Jonah 1 indicates that Jonah wished to flee from God's presence. Jonah 2:4 has him wishing to be in the presence of God. Are there times when you feel like Jonah, knowing that God's presence means joy and security and yet wanting to flee?

PRAYER IDEAS Thank God for his great love shown to you in Christ. Thank God that his mercy triumphs over his judgement, and that he forgives and rescues sinners like you and Jonah instead of giving you what you deserve.

The Lᴏʀᴅ said to Moses, "Cut for yourself two tablets of stone like the first, and I will write on the tablets the words that were on the first tablets, which you broke. ² Be ready by the morning, and come up in the morning to Mount Sinai, and present yourself there to

---

14. So they picked up Jonah and hurled him into the sea, and the sea ceased from its raging.

me on the top of the mountain. ³ No one shall come up with you, and let no one be seen throughout all the mountain. Let no flocks or herds graze opposite that mountain." ⁴ So Moses cut two tablets of stone like the first. And he rose early in the morning and went up on Mount Sinai, as the LORD had commanded him, and took in his hand two tablets of stone. ⁵ The LORD descended in the cloud and stood with him there, and proclaimed the name of the LORD. ⁶ The LORD passed before him and proclaimed, "The LORD, the LORD, a God merciful and gracious, slow to anger, and abounding in steadfast love and faithfulness, ⁷ keeping steadfast love for thousands, forgiving iniquity and transgression and sin, but who will by no means clear the guilty, visiting the iniquity of the fathers on the children and the children's children, to the third and the fourth generation." ⁸ And Moses quickly bowed his head toward the earth and worshiped. ⁹ And he said, "If now I have found favor in your sight, O Lord, please let the Lord go in the midst of us, for it is a stiff-necked people, and pardon our iniquity and our sin, and take us for your inheritance."

1. What remarkable things do you learn about God from this passage?

2. What is God's dominant desire in his actions towards his people?

3. Read John 1:14-18.¹⁵ How is God's revelation of himself in his Son the same as and/or different to his revelation to Moses?

PONDER How do you feel about the great mercy that God offers you in Jesus? Do you ever feel like God owes you something?

PRAYER IDEAS Ask God to help you to be thankful for what he has done for you in Jesus.

POINTER Exodus 34:6-8 is a key Old Testament passage. In Exodus 32-33, God changes his mind about a particular judgement he had announced upon his people. Exodus 34:6-8 explains that this action was in accord with God's character: he is the God of "steadfast love". In the Old Testament, the word for "steadfast love" is used to describe God's surprising, unexpected and overwhelming grace or love. Exodus 34:6-8, along with this special Old Testament word, is often echoed in the Old Testament (e.g. Joel 2:12-14¹⁶; Jonah 4:2¹⁷).

---

15. And the Word became flesh and dwelt among us, and we have seen his glory, glory as of the only Son from the Father, full of grace and truth. ¹⁵ (John bore witness about him, and cried out, "This was he of whom I said, 'He who comes after me ranks before me, because he was before me.'") ¹⁶ And from his fullness we have all received, grace upon grace. ¹⁷ For the law was given through Moses; grace and truth came through Jesus Christ. ¹⁸ No one has ever seen God; the only God, who is at the Father's side, he has made him known.
16. "Yet even now," declares the LORD,
"return to me with all your heart,
with fasting, with weeping, and with mourning;
¹³ and rend your hearts and not your garments."

Return to the LORD your God,
for he is gracious and merciful,
slow to anger, and abounding in steadfast love;
and he relents over disaster.
¹⁴ Who knows whether he will not turn and relent,
and leave a blessing behind him,
a grain offering and a drink offering
for the LORD your God?
17. And he prayed to the LORD and said, "O LORD, is not this what I said when I was yet in my country? That is why I made haste to flee to Tarshish; for I knew that you are a gracious God and merciful, slow to anger and abounding in steadfast love, and relenting from disaster."

LUKE 9-15

JONAH

2 TIMOTHY

Those who pay regard to vain idols forsake their hope of steadfast love.

The word for "steadfast love" that occurs in Exodus 34:6-8[18] and Jonah 4:2[19] also appears in Jonah 2:8.

1. What are the benefits of turning to God? What is forfeited if you do not turn to God, or if you turn away from him to idols?

2. Read 1 Thessalonians 1:9-10.[20] This passage talks about a group of people who have turned to God from idols. What benefit have they received?

PONDER Are you ever tempted to seek solace in things other than the God and Father of our Lord Jesus Christ? What would you forfeit in doing this?

PRAYER IDEAS Ask God to help you to keep being faithful to God. Pray for your friends and family: ask God to bring them to know him so that they might not miss out on the steadfast love that might be theirs.

Now the word of the LORD came to Jonah the son of Amittai, saying, 2 "Arise, go to Nineveh, that great city, and call out against it, for their evil has come up before me." 3 But Jonah rose to flee to Tarshish from the presence of the LORD. He went down to Joppa and found a ship going to Tarshish. So he paid the fare and went on board, to go with them to Tarshish, away from the presence of the LORD.
4 But the LORD hurled a great wind upon the sea, and there was a mighty tempest on the sea, so that the ship threatened to break up. 5 Then the mariners were afraid, and each cried out to his god. And they hurled the cargo that was in the ship into the sea to lighten it for them. But Jonah had gone down into the inner part of the ship and had lain down and was fast asleep. 6 So the captain came and said to him, "What do you mean, you sleeper? Arise, call out to your god! Perhaps the god will give a thought to us, that we may not perish."
7 And they said to one another, "Come, let us cast lots, that we may know on whose account this evil has come upon us." So they

---

18. The LORD passed before him and proclaimed, "The LORD, the LORD, a God merciful and gracious, slow to anger, and abounding in steadfast love and faithfulness, 7 keeping steadfast love for thousands, forgiving iniquity and transgression and sin, but who will by no means clear the guilty, visiting the iniquity of the fathers on the children and the children's children, to the third and the fourth generation." 8 And Moses quickly bowed his head toward the earth and worshiped.
19. And he prayed to the LORD and said, "O LORD, is not this what I said when I was yet in my country? That is why I made haste to flee to Tarshish; for I knew that you are a gracious God and merciful, slow to anger and abounding in steadfast love, and relenting from disaster."
20. For they themselves report concerning us the kind of reception we had among you, and how you turned to God from idols to serve the living and true God, 10 and to wait for his Son from heaven, whom he raised from the dead, Jesus who delivers us from the wrath to come.

cast lots, and the lot fell on Jonah. ⁸ Then they said to him, "Tell us on whose account this evil has come upon us. What is your occupation? And where do you come from? What is your country? And of what people are you?" ⁹ And he said to them, "I am a Hebrew, and I fear the LORD, the God of heaven, who made the sea and the dry land." ¹⁰ Then the men were exceedingly afraid and said to him, "What is this that you have done!" For the men knew that he was fleeing from the presence of the LORD, because he had told them.

¹¹ Then they said to him, "What shall we do to you, that the sea may quiet down for us?" For the sea grew more and more tempestuous. ¹² He said to them, "Pick me up and hurl me into the sea; then the sea will quiet down for you, for I know it is because of me that this great tempest has come upon you." ¹³ Nevertheless, the men rowed hard to get back to dry land, but they could not, for the sea grew more and more tempestuous against them. ¹⁴ Therefore they called out to the LORD, "O LORD, let us not perish for this man's life, and lay not on us innocent blood, for you, O LORD, have done as it pleased you." ¹⁵ So they picked up Jonah and hurled him into the sea, and the sea ceased from its raging. ¹⁶ Then the men feared the LORD exceedingly, and they offered a sacrifice to the LORD and made vows.

¹⁷ And the LORD appointed a great fish to swallow up Jonah. And Jonah was in the belly of the fish three days and three nights.

2:1 Then Jonah prayed to the LORD his God from the belly of the fish, ² saying,

"I called out to the LORD, out of my distress,
    and he answered me;
out of the belly of Sheol I cried,
    and you heard my voice.
³ For you cast me into the deep,
    into the heart of the seas,
    and the flood surrounded me;
all your waves and your billows
    passed over me.

⁴ Then I said, 'I am driven away
    from your sight;
yet I shall again look
    upon your holy temple.'
⁵ The waters closed in over me to take my
    life;
    the deep surrounded me;
weeds were wrapped about my head
    ⁶ at the roots of the mountains.
I went down to the land
    whose bars closed upon me forever;
yet you brought up my life from the pit,
    O LORD my God.
⁷ When my life was fainting away,
    I remembered the LORD,
and my prayer came to you,
    into your holy temple.
⁸ Those who pay regard to vain idols
    forsake their hope of steadfast love.
⁹ But I with the voice of thanksgiving
    will sacrifice to you;
what I have vowed I will pay.
    Salvation belongs to the LORD!"

¹⁰ And the LORD spoke to the fish, and it vomited Jonah out upon the dry land.

1. List the similarities between Jonah's experience and that of the mariners (e.g. both face a crisis from the sea).

2. Why do you think the author has recorded these similarities?

3. Read Jonah 2:9, Luke 19:10[21] and Romans 10:1-13[22] (vv. 12-13 especially). How does the book of Jonah prepare readers for what happens in the New Testament?

PONDER Consider your answer to question 3. What does this tell you about God's salvation priorities?

PRAYER IDEAS Praise God that "Salvation belongs to the LORD".

READING 31   PROVERBS 6:16-19, HABAKKUK 1:3, ECCLESIASTES 7:20

Proverbs 6:16-19

There are six things that the LORD hates, seven that are an abomination to him:
[17] haughty eyes, a lying tongue,
    and hands that shed innocent blood,
[18] a heart that devises wicked plans,
    feet that make haste to run to evil,
[19] a false witness who breathes out lies,
    and one who sows discord among
        brothers.

Habakkuk 1:3

Why do you make me see iniquity,
    and why do you idly look at wrong?
Destruction and violence are before me;
    strife and contention arise.

Ecclesiastes 7:20

Surely there is not a righteous man on earth who does good and never sins.

1. Jonah 1:9[23] says that God is the creator. Given that you are also his creation, what implication follows for how you are to relate to him?

2. Can anyone claim to be innocent of sin?

3. Why does God hate sin so much?

4. What can sinners expect from a holy God?

PONDER Examine the sin in your own life. Where do you feel you need to improve?

PRAYER IDEAS Thank God for being holy and for not overlooking sin. Thank him that because of Jesus, you can be rescued from his anger.

---

21. "For the Son of Man came to seek and to save the lost."
22. Brothers, my heart's desire and prayer to God for them is that they may be saved. 2 For I bear them witness that they have a zeal for God, but not according to knowledge. 3 For, being ignorant of the righteousness of God, and seeking to establish their own, they did not submit to God's righteousness. 4 For Christ is the end of the law for righteousness to everyone who believes.
5 For Moses writes about the righteousness that is based on the law, that the person who does the commandments shall live by them. 6 But the righteousness based on faith says, "Do not say in your heart, 'Who will ascend into heaven?'" (that is, to bring Christ down) 7 or "'Who will descend into the abyss?'" (that is, to bring Christ up from the dead). 8 But what does it say? "The word is near you, in your mouth and in your heart" (that is, the word of faith that we proclaim); 9 because, if you confess with your mouth that Jesus is Lord and believe in your heart that God raised him from the dead, you will be saved. 10 For with the heart one believes and is justified, and with the mouth one confesses and is saved. 11 For the Scripture says, "Everyone who believes in him will not be put to shame." 12 For there is no distinction between Jew and Greek; for the same Lord is Lord of all, bestowing his riches on all who call on him. 13 For "everyone who calls on the name of the Lord will be saved."
23. And he said to them, "I am a Hebrew, and I fear the LORD, the God of heaven, who made the sea and the dry land."

Then the word of the L ORD came to Jonah the second time, saying, ² "Arise, go to Nineveh, that great city, and call out against it the message that I tell you." ³ So Jonah arose and went to Nineveh, according to the word of the L ORD. Now Nineveh was an exceedingly great city, three days' journey in breadth. ⁴ Jonah began to go into the city, going a day's journey. And he called out, "Yet forty days, and Nineveh shall be overthrown!" ⁵ And the people of Nineveh believed God. They called for a fast and put on sackcloth, from the greatest of them to the least of them.

1. Where do you see evidence of God's steadfast love in this passage?

2. Where do you see evidence of God's anger at human sinfulness in this passage?

3. Nineveh was a 'three-day visit city' (see pointer below). How long did it take the Ninevites to respond?

PONDER Paul later reflects that he was the "foremost" of sinners and that God used his conversion as an example (1 Tim 1:15). Jonah 3:1-5 is another example of great and unexpected repentance. Do you believe God can turn such people to himself?

PRAYER IDEAS Pray for those whom you think are outside of God's help and beyond redemption.

POINTER Although Nineveh was undoubtedly a large city (Jonah 4:11 tells us that 120,000 people lived there), the "three days" may refer to the time it took for all the proper ancient protocols of such a major city to be observed. Alternatively, the phrase could imply that a prophetic visit took three days because it needed to ensure that the message was heard by the bulk of the population.

The word reached the king of Nineveh, and he arose from his throne, removed his robe, covered himself with sackcloth, and sat in ashes. ⁷ And he issued a proclamation and published through Nineveh, "By the decree of the king and his nobles: Let neither man nor beast, herd nor flock, taste anything. Let them not feed or drink water, ⁸ but let man and beast be covered with sackcloth, and let them call out mightily to God. Let everyone turn from his evil way and from the violence that is in his hands. ⁹ Who knows? God may turn

and relent and turn from his fierce anger, so that we may not perish."
¹⁰ When God saw what they did, how they turned from their evil way, God relented of the disaster that he had said he would do to them, and he did not do it.

1. How is the repentance of the Ninevites described?

LUKE 9:1-15

JONAH

2 TIMOTHY

2. How is their repentance expressed?

3. What indications are there that their repentance is genuine?

PONDER **PONDER** What are the similarities between the repentance you see here and in 2 Corinthians 7:5-13?[24] Is your repentance lacking? Why?

PRAYER IDEAS Ask God to give you a better grasp of his holiness.

READING 34   JONAH 3:10, JEREMIAH 18:8-10

Jonah 3:10

When God saw what they did, how they turned from their evil way, God relented of the disaster that he had said he would do to them, and he did not do it.

Jeremiah 18:8-10

... and if that nation, concerning which I have spoken, turns from its evil, I will relent of the disaster that I intended to do to it. 9 And if at any time I declare concerning a nation or a kingdom that I will build and plant it, 10 and if it does evil in my sight, not listening to my voice, then I will relent of the good that I had intended to do to it.

1. What does it mean in Jonah 3:10 and Jeremiah 18:8 when it says that God 'relented'?

2. Does this threaten your view of God or is it an encouragement? Why?

PONDER Do you think your prayers can affect how God acts in his world? Why/why not? What does this reveal about your view of God? Does this match the Scriptures' view of God?

PRAYER IDEAS Thank God for hearing your prayers and for considering them to be important to him. Ask him to make you more honest and diligent in prayer.

---

24. For even when we came into Macedonia, our bodies had no rest, but we were afflicted at every turn—fighting without and fear within. 6 But God, who comforts the downcast, comforted us by the coming of Titus, 7 and not only by his coming but also by the comfort with which he was comforted by you, as he told us of your longing, your mourning, your zeal for me, so that I rejoiced still more. 8 For even if I made you grieve with my letter, I do not regret it—though I did regret it, for I see that that letter grieved you, though only for a while. 9 As it is, I rejoice, not because you were grieved, but because you were grieved into repenting. For you felt a godly grief, so that you suffered no loss through us.

10 For godly grief produces a repentance that leads to salvation without regret, whereas worldly grief produces death. 11 For see what earnestness this godly grief has produced in you, but also what eagerness to clear yourselves, what indignation, what fear, what longing, what zeal, what punishment! At every point you have proved yourselves innocent in the matter. 12 So although I wrote to you, it was not for the sake of the one who did the wrong, nor for the sake of the one who suffered the wrong, but in order that your earnestness for us might be revealed to you in the sight of God. 13 Therefore we are comforted.

And besides our own comfort, we rejoiced still more at the joy of Titus, because his spirit has been refreshed by you all.

When God saw what they did, how they turned from their evil way, God relented of the disaster that he had said he would do to them, and he did not do it.

4:1 But it displeased Jonah exceedingly, and he was angry. ² And he prayed to the Lord and said, "O Lord, is not this what I said when I was yet in my country? That is why I made haste to flee to Tarshish; for I knew that you are a gracious God and merciful, slow to anger and abounding in steadfast love, and relenting from disaster. ³ Therefore now, O Lord, please take my life from me, for it is better for me to die than to live." ⁴ And the Lord said, "Do you do well to be angry?"

1. According to Jonah, why was he dis-obedient to God's initial call for him to go to Nineveh (4:2)?

2. Why do you think Jonah is displeased and angry?

3. What attitude does Jonah want God to have towards the following people:
a) himself?

b) God's people?

c) the nations?

PONDER Do you ever get angry when God acts one way towards you and then acts in the same way towards others? Why?

PRAYER IDEAS Ask God to form you in his likeness so that you will be as merciful, forgiving and accepting towards others as he is towards you.

Now the tax collectors and sinners were all drawing near to hear [Jesus]. ² And the Pharisees and the scribes grumbled, saying, "This man receives sinners and eats with them."

³ So he told them this parable: ⁴ "What man of you, having a hundred sheep, if he has lost one of them, does not leave the ninety-nine in the open country, and go after the one that is lost, until he finds it? ⁵ And when he has found it, he lays it on his shoulders, rejoicing. ⁶ And when he comes home, he calls together his friends and his neighbors, saying to them,

'Rejoice with me, for I have found my sheep that was lost.' ⁷ Just so, I tell you, there will be more joy in heaven over one sinner who repents than over ninety-nine righteous persons who need no repentance.

⁸ "Or what woman, having ten silver coins, if she loses one coin, does not light a lamp and sweep the house and seek diligently until she finds it? ⁹ And when she has found it, she calls together her friends and neighbors, saying, 'Rejoice with me, for I have found the coin that I had lost.' ¹⁰ Just so, I tell you, there is joy before the angels of God over one

sinner who repents."

¹¹ And he said, "There was a man who had two sons. ¹² And the younger of them said to his father, 'Father, give me the share of property that is coming to me.' And he divided his property between them. ¹³ Not many days later, the younger son gathered all he had and took a journey into a far country, and there he squandered his property in reckless living. ¹⁴ And when he had spent everything, a severe famine arose in that country, and he began to be in need. ¹⁵ So he went and hired himself out to one of the citizens of that country, who sent him into his fields to feed pigs. ¹⁶ And he was longing to be fed with the pods that the pigs ate, and no one gave him anything.

¹⁷ "But when he came to himself, he said, 'How many of my father's hired servants have more than enough bread, but I perish here with hunger! ¹⁸ I will arise and go to my father, and I will say to him, "Father, I have sinned against heaven and before you. ¹⁹ I am no longer worthy to be called your son. Treat me as one of your hired servants."' ²⁰ And he arose and came to his father. But while he was still a long way off, his father saw him and felt compassion, and ran and embraced him and kissed him. ²¹ And the son said to him, 'Father, I have sinned against heaven and before you. I am no longer worthy to be called your son.' ²² But the father said to his servants, 'Bring quickly the best robe, and put it on him, and put a ring on his hand, and shoes on his feet. ²³ And bring the fattened calf and kill it, and let us eat and celebrate. ²⁴ For this my son was dead, and is alive again; he was lost, and is found.' And they began to celebrate.

²⁵ "Now his older son was in the field, and as he came and drew near to the house, he heard music and dancing. ²⁶ And he called one of the servants and asked what these things meant. ²⁷ And he said to him, 'Your brother has come, and your father has killed the fattened calf, because he has received

him back safe and sound.' ²⁸ But he was angry and refused to go in. His father came out and entreated him, ²⁹ but he answered his father, 'Look, these many years I have served you, and I never disobeyed your command, yet you never gave me a young goat, that I might celebrate with my friends. ³⁰ But when this son of yours came, who has devoured your property with prostitutes, you killed the fattened calf for him!' ³¹ And he said to him, 'Son, you are always with me, and all that is mine is yours. ³² It was fitting to celebrate and be glad, for this your brother was dead, and is alive; he was lost, and is found.'"

1. What is the context of these parables? (Why is Jesus saying these things?)

2. How is the God you hear about in the book of Jonah like the father in third parable?

3. Which character in the third parable is most like Jonah?

PONDER What advice does Jesus give to people who think like Jonah?

PRAYER IDEAS Thank God for his keen desire to treat others the way he treats you—with mercy and grace.

Then Peter came up and said to him, "Lord, how often will my brother sin against me, and I forgive him? As many as seven times?" ²² Jesus said to him, "I do not say to you seven times, but seventy times seven.

²³ "Therefore the kingdom of heaven may be compared to a king who wished to settle accounts with his servants. ²⁴ When he began to settle, one was brought to him who owed him ten thousand talents. ²⁵ And since he could not pay, his master ordered him to be sold, with his wife and children and all that he had, and payment to be made. ²⁶ So the servant fell on his knees, imploring him, 'Have patience with me, and I will pay you everything.' ²⁷ And out of pity for him, the master of that servant released him and forgave him the debt. ²⁸ But when that same servant went out, he found one of his fellow servants who owed him a hundred denarii, and seizing him, he began to choke him, saying, 'Pay what you owe.' ²⁹ So his fellow servant fell down and pleaded with him, 'Have patience with me, and I will pay you.' ³⁰ He refused and went and put him in prison until he should pay the debt. ³¹ When his fellow servants saw what had taken place, they were greatly distressed, and they went and reported to their master all that had taken place. ³² Then his master summoned him and said to him, 'You wicked servant! I forgave you all that debt because you pleaded with me. ³³ And should not you have had mercy on your fellow servant, as I had mercy on you?' ³⁴ And in anger his master delivered him to the jailers, until he should pay all his debt. ³⁵ So also my heavenly Father will do to every one of you, if you do not forgive your brother from your heart."

1. *What similarities are there between Jonah and the unforgiving servant?*

2. *What is the essential sin committed by the unforgiving servant?*

3. *This passage illustrates one of the ways in which Christians can behave like Jonah. What are some others?*

PONDER What warning is there in this passage for those who persist in acting like Jonah? What consolation can you draw from the book of Jonah when you come up short the way Jonah does?

PRAYER IDEAS Thank God for continuing to forgive you as you continue to turn to him in repentance.

LUKE 9-15

JONAH

2 TIMOTHY

Jonah went out of the city and sat to the east of the city and made a booth for himself there. He sat under it in the shade, till he should see what would become of the city. ⁶ Now the LORD God appointed a plant and made it come up over Jonah, that it might be a shade over his head, to save him from his discomfort. So Jonah was exceedingly glad because of the plant. ⁷ But when dawn came up the next day, God appointed a worm that attacked the plant, so that it withered. ⁸ When the sun rose, God appointed a scorching east wind, and the sun beat down on the head of Jonah so that he was faint. And he asked that he might die and said, "It is better for me to die than to live." ⁹ But God said to Jonah, "Do you do well to be angry for the plant?" And he said, "Yes, I do well to be angry, angry enough to die." ¹⁰ And the LORD said, "You pity the plant, for which you did not labor, nor did you make it grow, which came into being in a night and perished in a night. ¹¹ And should not I pity Nineveh, that great city, in which there are more than 120,000 persons who do not know their right hand from their left, and also much cattle?"

1. Why is Jonah angry at God (cf. Reading 35)? How does he express his anger?

2. How does God act in response to Jonah's anger? What does God say in response to Jonah's anger?

3. What point is God making regarding the plant (vv. 10-11)?

PONDER Does God object to Jonah's anger or to his reasons for being angry? Is anger at God ever appropriate?

PRAYER IDEAS Thank God for his concern for the entire world. Ask him to give you a similar concern, reflected in your actions.

I lift up my eyes to the hills.
From where does my help come?
² My help comes from the LORD,
    who made heaven and earth.

³ He will not let your foot be moved;
    he who keeps you will not slumber.
⁴ Behold, he who keeps Israel
    will neither slumber nor sleep.

⁵ The LORD is your keeper;
    the LORD is your shade on your right
      hand.
⁶ The sun shall not strike you by day,
    nor the moon by night.

⁷ The LORD will keep you from all evil;
    he will keep your life.
⁸ The LORD will keep
    your going out and your coming in
    from this time forth and forevermore.

1. What does this passage tell you about God's nature?

2. How is it expressed towards his people?

3. In this psalm, what aspects of God's character remind you of the God you meet in the book of Jonah?

PONDER Where do you see the aspects of God's character mentioned in this psalm fulfilled in what God has done in Christ?

PRAYER IDEAS Turn Psalm 121 into a prayer thanking God for caring for his people and providing for them in Christ.

READING 40   WRAPPING THINGS UP

1. What have you learned about God, yourself and God's purpose in his world from studying the book of Jonah?

2. Which of these things has had the most impact on you?

PONDER How has what you've learned from the book of Jonah changed the way you live your life? What can you do to remind yourself of these things in the coming months?

PRAYER IDEAS Thank God for the Scriptures which not only testify to Christ, but teach, reprove, correct and train you in righteousness (John 5:39-40[25], 2 Tim 3:16[26]).

---

25. "You search the Scriptures because you think that in them you have eternal life; and it is they that bear witness about me, [40] yet you refuse to come to me that you may have life."

26. All Scripture is breathed out by God and profitable for teaching, for reproof, for correction, and for training in righteousness ...

2 TIMOTHY

INTRODUCTION

The last week you spend in any job is always frantic and usually involves things like tidying up your files, cleaning out your drawers and returning books. But the most important thing you need to do is equip your successor to take over your work. A well-executed handover is important for ensuring that your successor can do the job properly.

While writing 2 Timothy, Paul is aware that he may soon die (2 Tim 4:6-7, 18[27]). Paul has had a key role in the gospel of Jesus Christ going to the Gentiles, but he knows that it won't be too long before he will depart. In 2 Timothy, Paul writes his 'handover notes' for his younger colleague, Timothy. What do you think the apostle Paul will say to him? How will Paul equip Timothy for the future? Read on.

You might like to use this prayer (or your own variation of it) before each of the next 20 studies:

Dear God,
Thank you for the people you used to pass on the good news about your Son to each new generation and to me. As I read 2 Timothy, please increase my knowledge and love for you. Help me not to be ashamed of the good news in these last days.
Amen.

READING 41 — 2 TIMOTHY 1:1-2

Paul, an apostle of Christ Jesus by the will of God according to the promise of the life that is in Christ Jesus,

² To Timothy, my beloved child:

Grace, mercy, and peace from God the Father and Christ Jesus our Lord.

1. Who is Paul writing to?

2. What do we learn about Paul and Timothy, and the relationship between them in these verses? (See also Acts 16:1-5.[28])

---

27. For I am already being poured out as a drink offering, and the time of my departure has come. ⁷ I have fought the good fight, I have finished the race, I have kept the faith ... ¹⁸ The Lord will rescue me from every evil deed and bring me safely into his heavenly kingdom. To him be the glory forever and ever. Amen.
28. Paul came also to Derbe and to Lystra. A disciple was there, named Timothy, the son of a Jewish woman who was a believer, but his father was a Greek. ² He was well spoken of by the brothers at Lystra and Iconium. ³ Paul wanted Timothy to accompany him, and he took him and circumcised him because of the Jews who were in those places, for they all knew that his father was a Greek. ⁴ As they went on their way through the cities, they delivered to them for observance the decisions that had been reached by the apostles and elders who were in Jerusalem. ⁵ So the churches were strengthened in the faith, and they increased in numbers daily.

3. *How would you define the "[g]race, mercy, and peace from God the Father and Christ Jesus our Lord" that Paul speaks about?*

to a Christian elder (Timothy), not a Christian church. How might this affect the way you read the letter?

PRAYER IDEAS Thank God for sending Paul to carry the name of Jesus before the Gentiles (Acts 9:15[29]). Thank him for his grace and mercy towards you.

PONDER The letter of 2 Timothy is addressed

READING 42   ACTS 19:1-41 ■

And it happened that while Apollos was at Corinth, Paul passed through the inland country and came to Ephesus. There he found some disciples. 2 And he said to them, "Did you receive the Holy Spirit when you believed?" And they said, "No, we have not even heard that there is a Holy Spirit." 3 And he said, "Into what then were you baptized?" They said, "Into John's baptism." 4 And Paul said, "John baptized with the baptism of repentance, telling the people to believe in the one who was to come after him, that is, Jesus." 5 On hearing this, they were baptized in the name of the Lord Jesus. 6 And when Paul had laid his hands on them, the Holy Spirit came on them, and they began speaking in tongues and prophesying. 7 There were about twelve men in all.

8 And he entered the synagogue and for three months spoke boldly, reasoning and persuading them about the kingdom of God. 9 But when some became stubborn and continued in unbelief, speaking evil of the Way before the congregation, he withdrew from them and took the disciples with him, reasoning daily in the hall of Tyrannus. 10 This continued for two years, so that all the residents of Asia heard the word of the Lord, both Jews and Greeks.

11 And God was doing extraordinary miracles by the hands of Paul, 12 so that even handkerchiefs or aprons that had touched his skin were carried away to the sick, and their diseases left them and the evil spirits came out of them. 13 Then some of the itinerant Jewish exorcists undertook to invoke the name of the Lord Jesus over those who had evil spirits, saying, "I adjure you by the Jesus whom Paul proclaims." 14 Seven sons of a Jewish high priest named Sceva were doing this. 15 But the evil spirit answered them, "Jesus I know, and Paul I recognize, but who are you?" 16 And the man in whom was the evil spirit leaped on them, mastered all of them and overpowered them, so that they fled out of that house naked and wounded. 17 And this became known to all the residents of Ephesus, both Jews and Greeks. And fear fell upon them all, and the name of the Lord Jesus was extolled. 18 Also many of those who were now believers came, confessing and divulging their practices. 19 And a number of those who had practiced magic arts brought their books together and burned them in the sight of all. And they counted the value of them and found it came to fifty thousand pieces of silver. 20 So the word of the Lord continued to increase and prevail mightily.

21 Now after these events Paul resolved in the Spirit to pass through Macedonia and Achaia and go to Jerusalem, saying, "After I have been there, I must also see Rome." 22 And having sent into Macedonia two of his helpers, Timothy and Erastus, he himself

---

29. But the Lord said to him, "Go, for he is a chosen instrument of mine to carry my name before the Gentiles and kings and the children of Israel."

stayed in Asia for a while.

²³ About that time there arose no little disturbance concerning the Way. ²⁴ For a man named Demetrius, a silversmith, who made silver shrines of Artemis, brought no little business to the craftsmen. ²⁵ These he gathered together, with the workmen in similar trades, and said, "Men, you know that from this business we have our wealth. ²⁶ And you see and hear that not only in Ephesus but in almost all of Asia this Paul has persuaded and turned away a great many people, saying that gods made with hands are not gods. ²⁷ And there is danger not only that this trade of ours may come into disrepute but also that the temple of the great goddess Artemis may be counted as nothing, and that she may even be deposed from her magnificence, she whom all Asia and the world worship."

²⁸ When they heard this they were enraged and were crying out, "Great is Artemis of the Ephesians!" ²⁹ So the city was filled with the confusion, and they rushed together into the theater, dragging with them Gaius and Aristarchus, Macedonians who were Paul's companions in travel. ³⁰ But when Paul wished to go in among the crowd, the disciples would not let him. ³¹ And even some of the Asiarchs, who were friends of his, sent to him and were urging him not to venture into the theater. ³² Now some cried out one thing, some another, for the assembly was in confusion, and most of them did not know why they had come together. ³³ Some of the crowd prompted Alexander, whom the Jews had put forward. And Alexander, motioning with his hand, wanted to make a defense to the crowd. ³⁴ But when they recognized that he was a Jew, for about two hours they all cried out with one voice, "Great is Artemis of the Ephesians!"

³⁵ And when the town clerk had quieted the crowd, he said, "Men of Ephesus, who is there who does not know that the city of the Ephesians is temple keeper of the great Artemis, and of the sacred stone that fell from the sky? ³⁶ Seeing then that these things cannot be denied, you ought to be quiet and do nothing rash. ³⁷ For you have brought these men here who are neither sacrilegious nor blasphemers of our goddess. ³⁸ If therefore Demetrius and the craftsmen with him have a complaint against anyone, the courts are open, and there are proconsuls. Let them bring charges against one another. ³⁹ But if you seek anything further, it shall be settled in the regular assembly. ⁴⁰ For we really are in danger of being charged with rioting today, since there is no cause that we can give to justify this commotion." ⁴¹ And when he had said these things, he dismissed the assembly.

A number of verses in 2 Timothy suggest that Paul was writing from prison in Rome (1:16-17[30], 2:9[31], 4:16-17[32]) to Timothy who was in Ephesus (1:17-18[33], 4:12[34], 19[35]). Acts 19 describes how the city of Ephesus first heard about Jesus.

1. What does Acts 19:1-12 say about what Paul did in Ephesus?

---

30. May the Lord grant mercy to the household of Onesiphorus, for he often refreshed me and was not ashamed of my chains, ¹⁷ but when he arrived in Rome he searched for me earnestly and found me ...
31. ... for which I am suffering, bound with chains as a criminal. But the word of God is not bound!
32. At my first defense no one came to stand by me, but all deserted me. May it not be charged against them! ¹⁷ But the Lord stood by me and strengthened me, so that through me the message might be fully proclaimed and all the Gentiles might hear it. So I was rescued from the lion's mouth.
33. ... but when he arrived in Rome he searched for me earnestly and found me— ¹⁸ may the Lord grant him to find mercy from the Lord on that Day!—and you well know all the service he rendered at Ephesus.
34. Tychicus I have sent to Ephesus.
35. Greet Prisca and Aquila, and the household of Onesiphorus.

2. What does Acts 19:17-20 say about the people of Ephesus who became Christians?

3. What does Acts 19:23-41 say about the kind of city Ephesus was?

PONDER When the gospel came to Ephesus, it caused a riot because many people could see the change that the gospel would bring to their way of life. Compared to the culture you live in, what changes has the gospel brought to your way of life?

PRAYER IDEAS Thank God for the progress of "the word of the Lord" throughout the cities of the world. Ask him to reform the culture in your society through the transformation that comes with the gospel.

READING 43   2 TIMOTHY 1:3-5

I thank God whom I serve, as did my ancestors, with a clear conscience, as I remember you constantly in my prayers night and day. ⁴ As I remember your tears, I long to see you, that I may be filled with joy. ⁵ I am reminded of your sincere faith, a faith that dwelt first in your grandmother Lois and your mother Eunice and now, I am sure, dwells in you as well.

1. What does Paul give thanks for? (See also 2 Tim 3:14-15.³⁶)

2. Why do you think Paul is so deeply moved? (See also Acts 20:17-38 in the appendix, pp. 65-66.)

PONDER Paul was grateful for the "sincere faith" he saw in Timothy's life (v. 5). What might be the signs of sincere faith?

PRAYER IDEAS Thank God for Christian brothers and sisters that God has brought into your life. Ask him to increase their love and their trust in him so that they will demonstrate signs of a sincere faith.

READING 44   2 TIMOTHY 1:6-7

For this reason I remind you to fan into flame the gift of God, which is in you through the laying on of my hands, ⁷ for God gave us a spirit not of fear but of power and love and self-control.

1. Verse 6 begins with "For this reason". What

reason has Paul given in verses 3-5 (see Reading 43)?

---

36. But as for you, continue in what you have learned and have firmly believed, knowing from whom you learned it ¹⁵ and how from childhood you have been acquainted with the sacred writings, which are able to make you wise for salvation through faith in Christ Jesus.

2. How does verse 7 help explain what the "gift" in verse 6 is?

PONDER Why do you think Paul is against timidity in this context? (See also Mark 8:38.[37])

PRAYER IDEAS Ask God to give you boldness (not fear), love and self-control as you live among people who oppose Christ's lordship.

3. How might verse 7 have been an encouragement to Timothy?

READING 45   2 TIMOTHY 1:6-12

For this reason I remind you to fan into flame the gift of God, which is in you through the laying on of my hands, [7] for God gave us a spirit not of fear but of power and love and self-control. [8] Therefore do not be ashamed of the testimony about our Lord, nor of me his prisoner, but share in suffering for the gospel by the power of God, [9] who saved us and called us to a holy calling, not because of our works but because of his own purpose and grace, which he gave us in Christ Jesus before the ages began, [10] and which now has been manifested through the appearing of our Savior Christ Jesus, who abolished death and brought life and immortality to light through the gospel, [11] for which I was appointed a preacher and apostle and teacher, [12] which is why I suffer as I do. But I am not ashamed, for I know whom I have believed, and I am convinced that he is able to guard until that Day what has been entrusted to me.

1. Why does verse 8 flow logically out of verses 6-7?

2. List all the benefits that come to us through the gospel.

3. What have you contributed to your salvation and calling?

PONDER What are the consequences of not being ashamed of Jesus and his gospel (vv. 8, 12)? How does your zeal compare with Paul's?

PRAYER IDEAS Thank God that your salvation depends entirely on his kindness, not on your performance. Ask him to enable you to live out your "holy calling" until the day of Christ's return (v. 9).

---

37. "For whoever is ashamed of me and of my words in this adulterous and sinful generation, of him will the Son of Man also be ashamed when he comes in the glory of his Father with the holy angels."

LUKE 9-15

JONAH

2 TIMOTHY

Follow the pattern of the sound words that you have heard from me, in the faith and love that are in Christ Jesus. ¹⁴ By the Holy Spirit who dwells within us, guard the good deposit entrusted to you.

¹⁵ You are aware that all who are in Asia turned away from me, among whom are Phygelus and Hermogenes. ¹⁶ May the Lord grant mercy to the household of Onesiphorus, for he often refreshed me and was not ashamed of my chains, ¹⁷ but when he arrived in Rome he searched for me earnestly and found me— ¹⁸ may the Lord grant him to find mercy from the Lord on that Day!—and you well know all the service he rendered at Ephesus.

1. *Whose words should shape Timothy's ministry? What should Timothy do with them (vv. 13-14)?*

2. *What are Phygelus, Hermogenes and Onesiphorus examples of?*

PONDER To what extent is the good deposit of the gospel being guarded in your church and family context? How is it being guarded?

PRAYER IDEAS Ask God to enable you to guard the gospel through his Holy Spirit. Ask him to work in situations where apostolic teaching is not being rightly guarded and valued.

You then, my child, be strengthened by the grace that is in Christ Jesus, ² and what you have heard from me in the presence of many witnesses entrust to faithful men who will be able to teach others also. ³ Share in suffering as a good soldier of Christ Jesus. ⁴ No soldier gets entangled in civilian pursuits, since his aim is to please the one who enlisted him. ⁵ An athlete is not crowned unless he competes according to the rules. ⁶ It is the hard-working farmer who ought to have the first share of the crops. ⁷ Think over what I say, for the Lord will give you understanding in everything.

1. *What is Paul's desire for his teaching (v. 2)? Why? (See also 4:17.[38])*

2. *What do you learn about the grace mentioned in verse 1? (See also 1:2[39], 8-10.[40])*

---

38. But the Lord stood by me and strengthened me, so that through me the message might be fully proclaimed and all the Gentiles might hear it. So I was rescued from the lion's mouth.
39. To Timothy, my beloved child:
Grace, mercy, and peace from God the Father and Christ Jesus our Lord ...
40. Therefore do not be ashamed of the testimony about our Lord, nor of me his prisoner, but share in suffering for the gospel by the power of God, ⁹ who saved us and called us to a holy calling, not because of our works but because of his own purpose and grace, which he gave us in Christ Jesus before the ages began, ¹⁰ and which now has been manifested through the appearing of our Savior Christ Jesus, who abolished death and brought life and immortality to light through the gospel ...

3. What is it meant to do for Timothy? What does Timothy need this for (vv. 2-3)?

PONDER Paul uses three metaphors in verses 4-6: that of a soldier, an althete and a farmer. What do you think he is trying to say? How do these metaphors help Timothy's role as an elder?

PRAYER IDEAS Pray for ministries you know of that are involved in passing on the treasures of the gospel to the next generation of Christian leaders. Pray also for Christian leaders you know who are facing hardships because of their ministry.

READING 48   2 TIMOTHY 2:8-13

Remember Jesus Christ, risen from the dead, the offspring of David, as preached in my gospel, ⁹ for which I am suffering, bound with chains as a criminal. But the word of God is not bound! ¹⁰ Therefore I endure everything for the sake of the elect, that they also may obtain the salvation that is in Christ Jesus with eternal glory. ¹¹ The saying is trustworthy, for:

If we have died with him, we will also live with him;
¹² if we endure, we will also reign with him;
if we deny him, he also will deny us;
¹³ if we are faithless, he remains faithful—

for he cannot deny himself.

1. How is verse 8 a fitting summary of Paul's gospel? (See also Acts 26:19-29 in the appendix, p. 66.)

2. Does Paul come across as being frustrated by his chains? Why or why not?

3. What do verses 11-13 say about the Christian's status in Christ? (See also Matt 10:32-33.⁴¹)

PONDER Why do you think Paul needs to remind Timothy to "[r]emember Jesus Christ, risen from the dead, the offspring of David" (v. 8)?

PRAYER IDEAS Thank God that his word is not chained by human opposition. Ask him to keep you faithful to Jesus every day.

---

41. "So everyone who acknowledges me before men, I also will acknowledge before my Father who is in heaven, ³³ but whoever denies me before men, I also will deny before my Father who is in heaven."

Remind them of these things, and charge them before God not to quarrel about words, which does no good, but only ruins the hearers. [15] Do your best to present yourself to God as one approved, a worker who has no need to be ashamed, rightly handling the word of truth. [16] But avoid irreverent babble, for it will lead people into more and more ungodliness, [17] and their talk will spread like gangrene. Among them are Hymenaeus and Philetus, [18] who have swerved from the truth, saying that the resurrection has already happened. They are upsetting the faith of some. [19] But God's firm foundation stands, bearing this seal: "The Lord knows those who are his," and, "Let everyone who names the name of the Lord depart from iniquity."

1. What is Timothy to remind the church in Ephesus of? (Look back over your answers to Reading 48.)

2. In verse 14, Paul discourages quarrelling about words. But in verse 15, Paul encourages Timothy to handle the word of truth correctly. What is the difference?

3. What do those who belong to the Lord do?

PONDER According to Paul, the results of 'poor' teaching include the ruining of the hearers (v. 14), ungodliness (v. 16), and the upsetting of faith (v. 18). How does this help you recognize and assess 'poor' teaching?

PRAYER IDEAS Pray for your Christian leaders and teachers: ask God to help them to handle the word of truth rightly. In addition, ask him to strengthen you to "depart from iniquity" (v. 19).

2 Timothy 2:19

But God's firm foundation stands, bearing this seal: "The Lord knows those who are his," and, "Let everyone who names the name of the Lord depart from iniquity."

Numbers 16

Now Korah the son of Izhar, son of Kohath, son of Levi, and Dathan and Abiram the sons of Eliab, and On the son of Peleth, sons of Reuben, took men. [2] And they rose up before Moses, with a number of the people of Israel, 250 chiefs of the congregation, chosen from the assembly, well-known men. [3] They assembled themselves together against Moses and against Aaron and said to them, "You have gone too far! For all in the congregation are holy, every one of them, and the LORD is among them. Why then do you exalt yourselves above the assembly of the LORD?" [4] When Moses heard it, he fell on his face, [5] and he said to Korah and all his company, "In the morning the LORD will show who is his, and who is holy, and will bring him near to him. The one whom he chooses he will bring near to him. [6] Do this: take censers, Korah and all his company; [7] put fire in them and put incense on them before the

LORD tomorrow, and the man whom the LORD chooses shall be the holy one. You have gone too far, sons of Levi!" [8] And Moses said to Korah, "Hear now, you sons of Levi: [9] is it too small a thing for you that the God of Israel has separated you from the congregation of Israel, to bring you near to himself, to do service in the tabernacle of the LORD and to stand before the congregation to minister to them, [10] and that he has brought you near him, and all your brothers the sons of Levi with you? And would you seek the priesthood also? [11] Therefore it is against the LORD that you and all your company have gathered together. What is Aaron that you grumble against him?"

[12] And Moses sent to call Dathan and Abiram the sons of Eliab, and they said, "We will not come up. [13] Is it a small thing that you have brought us up out of a land flowing with milk and honey, to kill us in the wilderness, that you must also make yourself a prince over us? [14] Moreover, you have not brought us into a land flowing with milk and honey, nor given us inheritance of fields and vineyards. Will you put out the eyes of these men? We will not come up." [15] And Moses was very angry and said to the LORD, "Do not respect their offering. I have not taken one donkey from them, and I have not harmed one of them."

[16] And Moses said to Korah, "Be present, you and all your company, before the LORD, you and they, and Aaron, tomorrow. [17] And let every one of you take his censer and put incense on it, and every one of you bring before the LORD his censer, 250 censers; you also, and Aaron, each his censer." [18] So every man took his censer and put fire in them and laid incense on them and stood at the entrance of the tent of meeting with Moses and Aaron. [19] Then Korah assembled all the congregation against them at the entrance of the tent of meeting. And the glory of the LORD appeared to all the congregation. [20] And the LORD spoke to Moses and to Aaron, saying, [21] "Separate yourselves from among this congregation, that I may consume them in a moment." [22] And they fell on their faces and said, "O God, the God of the spirits of all flesh, shall one man sin, and will you be angry with all the congregation?" [23] And the LORD spoke to Moses, saying, [24] "Say to the congregation, Get away from the dwelling of Korah, Dathan, and Abiram."

[25] Then Moses rose and went to Dathan and Abiram, and the elders of Israel followed him. [26] And he spoke to the congregation, saying, "Depart, please, from the tents of these wicked men, and touch nothing of theirs, lest you be swept away with all their sins." [27] So they got away from the dwelling of Korah, Dathan, and Abiram. And Dathan and Abiram came out and stood at the door of their tents, together with their wives, their sons, and their little ones. [28] And Moses said, "Hereby you shall know that the LORD has sent me to do all these works, and that it has not been of my own accord. [29] If these men die as all men die, or if they are visited by the fate of all mankind, then the LORD has not sent me. [30] But if the LORD creates something new, and the ground opens its mouth and swallows them up with all that belongs to them, and they go down alive into Sheol, then you shall know that these men have despised the LORD."

[31] And as soon as he had finished speaking all these words, the ground under them split apart. [32] And the earth opened its mouth and swallowed them up, with their households and all the people who belonged to Korah and all their goods. [33] So they and all that belonged to them went down alive into Sheol, and the earth closed over them, and they perished from the midst of the assembly. [34] And all Israel who were around them fled at their cry, for they said, "Lest the earth swallow us up!" [35] And fire came out from the LORD and consumed the 250 men offering the incense.

[36] Then the LORD spoke to Moses, saying, [37] "Tell Eleazar the son of Aaron the priest

to take up the censers out of the blaze. Then scatter the fire far and wide, for they have become holy. [38] As for the censers of these men who have sinned at the cost of their lives, let them be made into hammered plates as a covering for the altar, for they offered them before the Lord, and they became holy. Thus they shall be a sign to the people of Israel." [39] So Eleazar the priest took the bronze censers, which those who were burned had offered, and they were hammered out as a covering for the altar, [40] to be a reminder to the people of Israel, so that no outsider, who is not of the descendants of Aaron, should draw near to burn incense before the Lord, lest he become like Korah and his company—as the Lord said to him through Moses.

[41] But on the next day all the congregation of the people of Israel grumbled against Moses and against Aaron, saying, "You have killed the people of the Lord." [42] And when the congregation had assembled against Moses and against Aaron, they turned toward the tent of meeting. And behold, the cloud covered it, and the glory of the Lord appeared. [43] And Moses and Aaron came to the front of the tent of meeting, [44] and the Lord spoke to Moses, saying, [45] "Get away from the midst of this congregation, that I may consume them in a moment." And they fell on their faces. [46] And Moses said to Aaron, "Take your censer, and put fire on it from off the altar and lay incense on it and carry it quickly to the congregation and make atonement for them, for wrath has gone out from the Lord; the plague has begun." [47] So Aaron took it as Moses said and ran into the midst of the assembly. And behold, the plague had already begun among the people. And he put on the incense and made atonement for the people. [48] And he stood between the dead and the living, and the plague was stopped. [49] Now those who died in the plague were 14,700, besides those who died in the affair of Korah. [50] And Aaron returned to Moses at the entrance of the tent of meeting, when the plague was stopped.

Numbers 16:5 is referred to in 2 Timothy 2:19.

1. Summarize the key conflict in Numbers 16.

2. By referring to Numbers 16:5 in 2 Timothy 2:19, Paul is making a striking claim about his own authority. What claim is he making?

3. What other encouragement for Timothy does Paul draw out of Numbers?

PONDER Even though we can't identify ourselves completely with Moses or Paul, what encouragement can we derive from these passage if we believe Paul's message?

PRAYER IDEAS Thank God for protecting his message from attack. Ask him to give you certainty of his truth.

But God's firm foundation stands, bearing this seal: "The Lord knows those who are his," and, "Let everyone who names the name of the Lord depart from iniquity."

[20] Now in a great house there are not only vessels of gold and silver but also of wood and clay, some for honorable use, some for dishonorable. [21] Therefore, if anyone cleanses himself from what is dishonorable, he will be a vessel for honorable use, set apart as holy, useful to the master of the house, ready for every good work.

[22] So flee youthful passions and pursue righteousness, faith, love, and peace, along with those who call on the Lord from a pure heart. [23] Have nothing to do with foolish, ignorant controversies; you know that they breed quarrels. [24] And the Lord's servant must not be quarrelsome but kind to everyone, able to teach, patiently enduring evil, [25] correcting his opponents with gentleness. God may perhaps grant them repentance leading to a knowledge of the truth, [26] and they may come to their senses and escape from the snare of the devil, after being captured by him to do his will.

1. What is the connection between verse 19 and verses 20-21?

2. What is Timothy to flee from? What is he to flee to?

3. How is Timothy to deal with those who oppose him? What goal should Timothy have in mind?

PONDER In verses 21 and following, Paul urges Timothy to be godly ('cleansed'). Why is this important for Timothy's ministry?

PRAYER IDEAS Use verse 22 as the basis for prayerful reflection on your own life.

Behold my servant, whom I uphold,
my chosen, in whom my soul delights;
I have put my Spirit upon him;
    he will bring forth justice to the nations.
[2] He will not cry aloud or lift up his voice,
    or make it heard in the street;
[3] a bruised reed he will not break,
    and a faintly burning wick he will not
      quench;
    he will faithfully bring forth justice.

[4] He will not grow faint or be discouraged
    till he has established justice in the
      earth;
    and the coastlands wait for his law.

1. 2 Timothy 2:24 refers to the "Lord's servant"[42], an expression which has been taken from the book of Isaiah—particularly chapter 42. Fill out your picture of the Lord's servant from Isaiah 42:1-4. What

---

42. And the Lord's servant must not be quarrelsome but kind to everyone, able to teach, patiently enduring evil ...

is he like? According to these verses, how will the Lord's servant respond to his enemies?

52:13–53:12 in the appendix on pp. 66–67 for further clues.)

PONDER What aspects of Jesus' life help you to know how to respond to false teachers?

PRAYER IDEAS Ask God to give you the strength and the perseverance to follow the example of Timothy, Paul and Jesus.

2. Who is the ultimate servant of the Lord? (You may like to refer to Isaiah

READING 53   2 TIMOTHY 3:1-9

But understand this, that in the last days there will come times of difficulty. 2 For people will be lovers of self, lovers of money, proud, arrogant, abusive, disobedient to their parents, ungrateful, unholy, 3 heartless, unappeasable, slanderous, without self-control, brutal, not loving good, 4 treacherous, reckless, swollen with conceit, lovers of pleasure rather than lovers of God, 5 having the appearance of godliness, but denying its power. Avoid such people. 6 For among them are those who creep into households and capture weak women, burdened with sins and led astray by various passions, 7 always learning and never able to arrive at a knowledge of the truth. 8 Just as Jannes and Jambres opposed Moses, so these men also oppose the truth, men corrupted in mind and disqualified regarding the faith. 9 But they will not get very far, for their folly will be plain to all, as was that of those two men.

1. Are you living in the "last days" now (v. 1)? (See also Acts 2:16-21.[43])

2. How does Paul describes life in the "last days"?

3. The people of verses 2-4 have the appearance of godliness, but they deny its power (v. 5). What do you think the mere outward appearance of godliness lacks the power to do?

---

43. But this is what was uttered through the prophet Joel:

17 "'And in the last days it shall be, God declares,
that I will pour out my Spirit on all flesh,
and your sons and your daughters shall prophesy,
    and your young men shall see visions,
    and your old men shall dream dreams;
18 even on my male servants and female servants
    in those days I will pour out my Spirit, and they shall
        prophesy.
19 And I will show wonders in the heavens above

and signs on the earth below,
blood, and fire, and vapor of smoke;
20 the sun shall be turned to darkness
and the moon to blood,
before the day of the Lord comes, the great and
    magnificent day.
21 And it shall come to pass that everyone who calls upon
    the name of the Lord shall be saved.'"

PONDER To what extent do verses 2-5 describe the people in your society? Are these "times of difficulty" difficult for the Christian or the non-Christian (v. 1)?

PRAYER IDEAS Pray for people around you who not only live *in* the last days, but *for* the last days. Ask God to soften their hearts so that they will live for Jesus, the King of the last days.

POINTER v. 8: You won't find the names 'Jannes' and 'Jambres' in the Old Testament. However, the Egyptian sorcerers who opposed Moses before Pharaoh (Exod 7:11-24—see the appendix, pp. 67-68) were called 'Jannes' and 'Jambres' in non-biblical Jewish writings.

READING 54   2 TIMOTHY 3:10-13 ☐

You, however, have followed my teaching, my conduct, my aim in life, my faith, my patience, my love, my steadfastness, [11] my persecutions and sufferings that happened to me at Antioch, at Iconium, and at Lystra—which persecutions I endured; yet from them all the Lord rescued me. [12] Indeed, all who desire to live a godly life in Christ Jesus will be persecuted, [13] while evil people and impostors will go on from bad to worse, deceiving and being deceived.

1. How did Timothy 'follow' Paul's teaching (v. 10)? (See also Acts 16:1-5.[44])

2. What did it cost Paul, the apostle of

Christ, to follow Christ?

3. What is God's promise to you in verse 12?

PONDER Why does a desire to live a godly life in these "last days" (2 Tim 3:1) bring persecution to Christians (v. 12)?

PRAYER IDEAS Pray for Christian brothers and sisters you know (or know of) who face daily persecution for being Christian. Pray also for Christians who face the more subtle pressure of conforming to the character of the "last days": ask God to help them to continue to be godly.

READING 55   2 TIMOTHY 3:14-17 ☐

But as for you, continue in what you have learned and have firmly believed, knowing from whom you learned it [15] and how from childhood you have been acquainted with the sacred writings, which are able to make you wise for salvation through faith in Christ Jesus. [16] All Scripture is breathed out by God and profitable for teaching, for reproof, for correction, and for training in righteousness, [17] that the man of God may be competent, equipped for every good work.

---

44. Paul came also to Derbe and to Lystra. A disciple was there, named Timothy, the son of a Jewish woman who was a believer, but his father was a Greek. [2] He was well spoken of by the brothers at Lystra and Iconium. [3] Paul wanted Timothy to accompany him, and he took him and circumcised him because of the Jews who were in those places, for they all knew that his father was a Greek. [4] As they went on their way through the cities, they delivered to them for observance the decisions that had been reached by the apostles and elders who were in Jerusalem. [5] So the churches were strengthened in the faith, and they increased in numbers daily.

1. What is Timothy to continue in?

2. What are the "sacred writings" able to achieve (v. 15)? How does this compare to what Paul speaks of in verse 5?[45]

3. What is Scripture useful for?

4. Who is the "man of God" (v. 17)?

PONDER Some say that a focus on 'Scripture alone' leads only to head knowledge. From verses 16-17, how would you respond to this statement?

PRAYER IDEAS Thank God that the Bible is able to make you wise for salvation and to equip you for righteousness. Ask him to keep on showing you from the Bible the areas of your life that need to change.

POINTER In verses 15-16, Paul uses two different terms: "the sacred writings" (v. 15) and "Scripture" (v. 16). The phrase "sacred writings" was used among Greek-speaking Jews (like Timothy) to refer to the Old Testament. The term "Scripture" literally means 'writing', but is used by New Testament authors to refer exclusively to the Old Testament. However, by the time of Paul's day, Christians were beginning to consider some Christian writings as "Scripture", and therefore thought they possessed the same authority as the Old Testament (e.g. in 2 Peter 3:16[46], Peter refers to Paul's writings as 'Scripture'; in 1 Timothy 5:18[47], Paul refers to the words of Jesus in Luke 10:7[48] as "Scripture").

READING 56 · 2 TIMOTHY 4:1-5

I charge you in the presence of God and of Christ Jesus, who is to judge the living and the dead, and by his appearing and his kingdom: 2 preach the word; be ready in season and out of season; reprove, rebuke, and exhort, with complete patience and teaching. 3 For the time is coming when people will not endure sound teaching, but having itching ears they will accumulate for themselves teachers to suit their own passions, 4 and will turn away from listening to the truth and wander off into myths. 5 As for you, always be sober-minded, endure suffering, do the work of an evangelist, fulfill your ministry.

1. What charge does Paul give to Timothy the elder?

---

45. ... having the appearance of godliness, but denying its power. Avoid such people.
46. ... as he does in all his letters when he speaks in them of these matters. There are some things in them that are hard to understand, which the ignorant and unstable twist to their own destruction, as they do the other Scriptures.

47. For the Scripture says, "You shall not muzzle an ox when it treads out the grain," and, "The laborer deserves his wages."
48. "And remain in the same house, eating and drinking what they provide, for the laborer deserves his wages. Do not go from house to house."

2. What are the consequences of having "itching ears"?

teachers we appoint over us and the teaching we choose to receive?

PRAYER IDEAS Pray for your church leaders using verses 1-2 as the basis for your prayers. Ask God to save you from having "itching ears".

PONDER How should Paul's charge to Timothy influence our decisions about the

READING 57   2 TIMOTHY 4:6-8

For I am already being poured out as a drink offering, and the time of my departure has come. [7] I have fought the good fight, I have finished the race, I have kept the faith. [8] Henceforth there is laid up for me the crown of righteousness, which the Lord, the righteous judge, will award to me on that Day, and not only to me but also to all who have loved his appearing.

1. How does the second half of 2 Timothy 4:6 help you understand what Paul means when he says "I am already being poured out as a drink offering"? (Read Numbers 15:1-5[49] for an example of an Old Testament drink offering.)

2. What 'fights' and 'races' has Paul participated in (v. 7)?

3. What reward does Paul look forward to?

PONDER To what extent does verse 8 describe how you think about the coming "Day" of judgement?

PRAYER IDEAS Pray for any people you know who are wavering in their faith: ask God to give them perseverance.

READING 58   2 TIMOTHY 4:8-18

Henceforth there is laid up for me the crown of righteousness, which the Lord, the righteous judge, will award to me on that Day, and not only to me but also to all who have loved his appearing.

[9] Do your best to come to me soon. [10] For Demas, in love with this present world, has deserted me and gone to Thessalonica. Crescens has gone to Galatia, Titus to Dalmatia. [11] Luke alone is with me. Get Mark

49. The LORD spoke to Moses, saying, [2] "Speak to the people of Israel and say to them, When you come into the land you are to inhabit, which I am giving you, [3] and you offer to the LORD from the herd or from the flock a food offering or a burnt offering or a sacrifice, to fulfill a vow or as a freewill offering or at your appointed feasts, to make a pleasing aroma to the LORD, [4] then he who brings his offering shall offer to the LORD a grain offering of a tenth of an ephah of fine flour, mixed with a quarter of a hin of oil; [5] and you shall offer with the burnt offering, or for the sacrifice, a quarter of a hin of wine for the drink offering for each lamb."

LUKE 9-15

JONAH

2 TIMOTHY

and bring him with you, for he is very useful to me for ministry. [12] Tychicus I have sent to Ephesus. [13] When you come, bring the cloak that I left with Carpus at Troas, also the books, and above all the parchments. [14] Alexander the coppersmith did me great harm; the Lord will repay him according to his deeds. [15] Beware of him yourself, for he strongly opposed our message. [16] At my first defense no one came to stand by me, but all deserted me. May it not be charged against them! [17] But the Lord stood by me and strengthened me, so that through me the message might be fully proclaimed and all the Gentiles might hear it. So I was rescued from the lion's mouth. [18] The Lord will rescue me from every evil deed and bring me safely into his heavenly kingdom. To him be the glory forever and ever. Amen.

1. What two 'loves' are contrasted in verse 8 and verse 10?

2. What do verses 11-13 tell you about Paul?

3. Who supported Paul during his trials? Who did not?

PONDER How do you normally respond to the type of opposition Paul describes in verse 14?

PRAYER IDEAS Ask God to strengthen you so that you will stand firm in the face of opposition from friends or workmates.

READING 59   2 TIMOTHY 4:19-22

Greet Prisca and Aquila, and the household of Onesiphorus. [20] Erastus remained at Corinth, and I left Trophimus, who was ill, at Miletus. [21] Do your best to come before winter. Eubulus sends greetings to you, as do Pudens and Linus and Claudia and all the brothers.
[22] The Lord be with your spirit. Grace be with you.

1. *What does the incidental reference for Timothy to "come before winter" tell us about Paul (v. 21)? (See also 4:13 in Reading 58.)*

2. *Verse 22 literally says "Grace be with you [plural]". Other than Timothy, who would 'you' include?*

3. *Why do you think Timothy would have needed this encouragement?*

PONDER Paul concludes his letter with "Grace be with you". How does recognizing God's unmerited favour, forgiveness and enabling power affect your day-to-day living? (See also 2 Tim 1:9-10.[50])

---

50. ... who saved us and called us to a holy calling, not because of our works but because of his own purpose and grace, which he gave us in Christ Jesus before the ages began,

[10] and which now has been manifested through the appearing of our Savior Christ Jesus, who abolished death and brought life and immortality to light through the gospel ...

for, his abundant generosity to you. (See also
Eph 3:17-19.[51])

READING 60   2 TIMOTHY 1-4

Paul, an apostle of Christ Jesus by the will
of God according to the promise of the
life that is in Christ Jesus,

2 To Timothy, my beloved child:

Grace, mercy, and peace from God the
Father and Christ Jesus our Lord.

3 I thank God whom I serve, as did my
ancestors, with a clear conscience, as I
remember you constantly in my prayers night
and day. 4 As I remember your tears, I long to
see you, that I may be filled with joy. 5 I am
reminded of your sincere faith, a faith that
dwelt first in your grandmother Lois and your
mother Eunice and now, I am sure, dwells in
you as well. 6 For this reason I remind you to
fan into flame the gift of God, which is in you
through the laying on of my hands, 7 for God
gave us a spirit not of fear but of power and
love and self-control.

8 Therefore do not be ashamed of the
testimony about our Lord, nor of me his
prisoner, but share in suffering for the gospel
by the power of God, 9 who saved us and
called us to a holy calling, not because of our
works but because of his own purpose and
grace, which he gave us in Christ Jesus before
the ages began, 10 and which now has been
manifested through the appearing of our
Savior Christ Jesus, who abolished death and
brought life and immortality to light through
the gospel, 11 for which I was appointed a
preacher and apostle and teacher, 12 which is
why I suffer as I do. But I am not ashamed,
for I know whom I have believed, and I am
convinced that he is able to guard until that
Day what has been entrusted to me. 13 Follow
the pattern of the sound words that you

have heard from me, in the faith and love
that are in Christ Jesus. 14 By the Holy Spirit
who dwells within us, guard the good deposit
entrusted to you.

15 You are aware that all who are in Asia
turned away from me, among whom are
Phygelus and Hermogenes. 16 May the Lord
grant mercy to the household of Onesiphorus,
for he often refreshed me and was not
ashamed of my chains, 17 but when he arrived
in Rome he searched for me earnestly and
found me— 18 may the Lord grant him to
find mercy from the Lord on that Day!—and
you well know all the service he rendered at
Ephesus.

2:1 You then, my child, be strengthened by
the grace that is in Christ Jesus, 2 and what
you have heard from me in the presence of
many witnesses entrust to faithful men who
will be able to teach others also. 3 Share in
suffering as a good soldier of Christ Jesus.
4 No soldier gets entangled in civilian pursuits,
since his aim is to please the one who enlisted
him. 5 An athlete is not crowned unless he
competes according to the rules. 6 It is the
hard-working farmer who ought to have the
first share of the crops. 7 Think over what I
say, for the Lord will give you understanding
in everything.

8 Remember Jesus Christ, risen from the
dead, the offspring of David, as preached in
my gospel, 9 for which I am suffering, bound
with chains as a criminal. But the word of
God is not bound! 10 Therefore I endure
everything for the sake of the elect, that
they also may obtain the salvation that is in
Christ Jesus with eternal glory. 11 The saying is

LUKE 9-15

JONAH

2 TIMOTHY

---

51. ... so that Christ may dwell in your hearts through
faith—that you, being rooted and grounded in love, 18 may have
strength to comprehend with all the saints what is the breadth

and length and height and depth, 19 and to know the love of
Christ that surpasses knowledge, that you may be filled with all
the fullness of God.

trustworthy, for:

If we have died with him, we will also live
  with him;
12 if we endure, we will also reign with him;
if we deny him, he also will deny us;
13 if we are faithless, he remains faithful—

for he cannot deny himself.

14 Remind them of these things, and charge
them before God not to quarrel about words,
which does no good, but only ruins the
hearers. 15 Do your best to present yourself
to God as one approved, a worker who has
no need to be ashamed, rightly handling the
word of truth. 16 But avoid irreverent babble,
for it will lead people into more and more
ungodliness, 17 and their talk will spread
like gangrene. Among them are Hymenaeus
and Philetus, 18 who have swerved from the
truth, saying that the resurrection has already
happened. They are upsetting the faith of
some. 19 But God's firm foundation stands,
bearing this seal: "The Lord knows those who
are his," and, "Let everyone who names the
name of the Lord depart from iniquity."

20 Now in a great house there are not only
vessels of gold and silver but also of wood
and clay, some for honorable use, some for
dishonorable. 21 Therefore, if anyone cleanses
himself from what is dishonorable, he will be
a vessel for honorable use, set apart as holy,
useful to the master of the house, ready for
every good work.

22 So flee youthful passions and pursue
righteousness, faith, love, and peace, along
with those who call on the Lord from a pure
heart. 23 Have nothing to do with foolish,
ignorant controversies; you know that they
breed quarrels. 24 And the Lord's servant must
not be quarrelsome but kind to everyone, able
to teach, patiently enduring evil, 25 correcting
his opponents with gentleness. God may
perhaps grant them repentance leading to a
knowledge of the truth, 26 and they may come
to their senses and escape from the snare of
the devil, after being captured by him to do
his will.

3:1 But understand this, that in the last
days there will come times of difficulty. 2 For
people will be lovers of self, lovers of money,
proud, arrogant, abusive, disobedient to
their parents, ungrateful, unholy, 3 heartless,
unappeasable, slanderous, without self-
control, brutal, not loving good, 4 treacherous,
reckless, swollen with conceit, lovers of
pleasure rather than lovers of God, 5 having
the appearance of godliness, but denying
its power. Avoid such people. 6 For among
them are those who creep into households
and capture weak women, burdened with
sins and led astray by various passions,
7 always learning and never able to arrive at a
knowledge of the truth. 8 Just as Jannes and
Jambres opposed Moses, so these men also
oppose the truth, men corrupted in mind and
disqualified regarding the faith. 9 But they
will not get very far, for their folly will be
plain to all, as was that of those two men.

10 You, however, have followed my teaching,
my conduct, my aim in life, my faith, my
patience, my love, my steadfastness, 11 my
persecutions and sufferings that happened
to me at Antioch, at Iconium, and at Lystra—
which persecutions I endured; yet from them
all the Lord rescued me. 12 Indeed, all who
desire to live a godly life in Christ Jesus will be
persecuted, 13 while evil people and impostors
will go on from bad to worse, deceiving and
being deceived. 14 But as for you, continue
in what you have learned and have firmly
believed, knowing from whom you learned
it 15 and how from childhood you have been
acquainted with the sacred writings, which are
able to make you wise for salvation through
faith in Christ Jesus. 16 All Scripture is breathed
out by God and profitable for teaching, for
reproof, for correction, and for training in
righteousness, 17 that the man of God may be
competent, equipped for every good work.

4:1 I charge you in the presence of God
and of Christ Jesus, who is to judge the

living and the dead, and by his appearing and his kingdom: 2 preach the word; be ready in season and out of season; reprove, rebuke, and exhort, with complete patience and teaching. 3 For the time is coming when people will not endure sound teaching, but having itching ears they will accumulate for themselves teachers to suit their own passions, 4 and will turn away from listening to the truth and wander off into myths. 5 As for you, always be sober-minded, endure suffering, do the work of an evangelist, fulfill your ministry.

6 For I am already being poured out as a drink offering, and the time of my departure has come. 7 I have fought the good fight, I have finished the race, I have kept the faith. 8 Henceforth there is laid up for me the crown of righteousness, which the Lord, the righteous judge, will award to me on that Day, and not only to me but also to all who have loved his appearing.

9 Do your best to come to me soon. 10 For Demas, in love with this present world, has deserted me and gone to Thessalonica. Crescens has gone to Galatia, Titus to Dalmatia. 11 Luke alone is with me. Get Mark and bring him with you, for he is very useful to me for ministry. 12 Tychicus I have sent to Ephesus. 13 When you come, bring the cloak that I left with Carpus at Troas, also the books, and above all the parchments. 14 Alexander the coppersmith did me great harm; the Lord will repay him according to his deeds. 15 Beware of him yourself, for he strongly opposed our message. 16 At my first defense no one came to stand by me, but all deserted me. May it not be charged against them! 17 But the Lord stood by me and strengthened me, so that through me the message might be fully proclaimed and all the Gentiles might hear it. So I was rescued from the lion's mouth. 18 The Lord will rescue me from every evil deed and bring me safely into his heavenly kingdom. To him be the glory forever and ever. Amen.

19 Greet Prisca and Aquila, and the household of Onesiphorus. 20 Erastus remained at Corinth, and I left Trophimus, who was ill, at Miletus. 21 Do your best to come before winter. Eubulus sends greetings to you, as do Pudens and Linus and Claudia and all the brothers.

22 The Lord be with your spirit. Grace be with you.

PONDER Looking back over 2 Timothy, how would you summarize Paul's message to Timothy?

PRAYER IDEAS Use 2 Timothy 1:13-14 as the basis for your prayer.

LUKE 9-15

JONAH

2 TIMOTHY

APPENDIX

ADDITIONAL PASSAGES REFERRED TO ...

Isaiah 6 (Reading 22)

In the year that King Uzziah died I saw the Lord sitting upon a throne, high and lifted up; and the train of his robe filled the temple. ² Above him stood the seraphim. Each had six wings: with two he covered his face, and with two he covered his feet, and with two he flew. ³ And one called to another and said:

"Holy, holy, holy is the Lᴏʀᴅ of hosts;
the whole earth is full of his glory!"

⁴ And the foundations of the thresholds shook at the voice of him who called, and the house was filled with smoke. ⁵ And I said: "Woe is me! For I am lost; for I am a man of unclean lips, and I dwell in the midst of a people of unclean lips; for my eyes have seen the King, the Lᴏʀᴅ of hosts!"

⁶ Then one of the seraphim flew to me, having in his hand a burning coal that he had taken with tongs from the altar. ⁷ And he touched my mouth and said: "Behold, this has touched your lips; your guilt is taken away, and your sin atoned for."

⁸ And I heard the voice of the Lord saying, "Whom shall I send, and who will go for us?" Then I said, "Here am I! Send me." ⁹ And he said, "Go, and say to this people:

"'Keep on hearing, but do not understand;
keep on seeing, but do not perceive.'
¹⁰ Make the heart of this people dull,
and their ears heavy,
and blind their eyes;
lest they see with their eyes,
and hear with their ears,
and understand with their hearts,
and turn and be healed."
¹¹ Then I said, "How long, O Lord?"
And he said:
"Until cities lie waste
without inhabitant,
and houses without people,
and the land is a desolate waste,
¹² and the Lᴏʀᴅ removes people far away,
and the forsaken places are many in the
midst of the land.
¹³ And though a tenth remain in it,
it will be burned again,
like a terebinth or an oak,
whose stump remains
when it is felled."
The holy seed is its stump.

Acts 20:17–38 (Reading 43)

Now from Miletus he sent to Ephesus and called the elders of the church to come to him. ¹⁸ And when they came to him, he said to them:

"You yourselves know how I lived among you the whole time from the first day that I set foot in Asia, ¹⁹ serving the Lord with all humility and with tears and with trials that happened to me through the plots of the Jews; ²⁰ how I did not shrink from declaring to you anything that was profitable, and teaching you in public and from house to house, ²¹ testifying both to Jews and to Greeks of repentance toward God and of faith in our Lord Jesus Christ. ²² And now, behold, I am going to Jerusalem, constrained by the Spirit, not knowing what will happen to me there, ²³ except that the

Holy Spirit testifies to me in every city that imprisonment and afflictions await me. 24 But I do not account my life of any value nor as precious to myself, if only I may finish my course and the ministry that I received from the Lord Jesus, to testify to the gospel of the grace of God. 25 And now, behold, I know that none of you among whom I have gone about proclaiming the kingdom will see my face again. 26 Therefore I testify to you this day that I am innocent of the blood of all of you, 27 for I did not shrink from declaring to you the whole counsel of God. 28 Pay careful attention to yourselves and to all the flock, in which the Holy Spirit has made you overseers, to care for the church of God, which he obtained with his own blood. 29 I know that after my departure fierce wolves will come in among you, not sparing the flock; 30 and from among your own selves will arise men speaking twisted things, to draw away the disciples after them. 31 Therefore be alert, remembering that for three years I did not cease night or day to admonish everyone with tears. 32 And now I commend you to God and to the word of his grace, which is able to build you up and to give you the inheritance among all those who are sanctified. 33 I coveted no one's silver or gold or apparel. 34 You yourselves know that these hands ministered to my necessities and to those who were with me. 35 In all things I have shown you that by working hard in this way we must help the weak and remember the words of the Lord Jesus, how he himself said, 'It is more blessed to give than to receive.'"

36 And when he had said these things, he knelt down and prayed with them all. 37 And there was much weeping on the part of all; they embraced Paul and kissed him, 38 being sorrowful most of all because of the word he had spoken, that they would not see his face again. And they accompanied him to the ship.

Acts 26:19-29 (Reading 48)

"Therefore, O King Agrippa, I was not disobedient to the heavenly vision, 20 but declared first to those in Damascus, then in Jerusalem and throughout all the region of Judea, and also to the Gentiles, that they should repent and turn to God, performing deeds in keeping with their repentance. 21 For this reason the Jews seized me in the temple and tried to kill me. 22 To this day I have had the help that comes from God, and so I stand here testifying both to small and great, saying nothing but what the prophets and Moses said would come to pass: 23 that the Christ must suffer and that, by being the first to rise from the dead, he would proclaim light both to our people and to the Gentiles."

24 And as he was saying these things in his defense, Festus said with a loud voice, "Paul, you are out of your mind; your great learning is driving you out of your mind." 25 But Paul said, "I am not out of my mind, most excellent Festus, but I am speaking true and rational words. 26 For the king knows about these things, and to him I speak boldly. For I am persuaded that none of these things has escaped his notice, for this has not been done in a corner. 27 King Agrippa, do you believe the prophets? I know that you believe." 28 And Agrippa said to Paul, "In a short time would you persuade me to be a Christian?" 29 And Paul said, "Whether short or long, I would to God that not only you but also all who hear me this day might become such as I am—except for these chains."

Isaiah 52:13-53:12 (Reading 52)

Behold, my servant shall act wisely;
    he shall be high and lifted up,
        and shall be exalted.
14 As many were astonished at you—
        his appearance was so marred, beyond
            human semblance,
        and his form beyond that of the
            children of mankind—

15 so shall he sprinkle many nations;
kings shall shut their mouths because
of him;
for that which has not been told them they
see,
and that which they have not heard
they understand.
53:1 Who has believed what he has heard
from us?
And to whom has the arm of the LORD
been revealed?
2 For he grew up before him like a young
plant,
and like a root out of dry ground;
he had no form or majesty that we should
look at him,
and no beauty that we should desire
him.
3 He was despised and rejected by men;
a man of sorrows, and acquainted with
grief;
and as one from whom men hide their faces
he was despised, and we esteemed him
not.

4 Surely he has borne our griefs
and carried our sorrows;
yet we esteemed him stricken,
smitten by God, and afflicted.
5 But he was wounded for our
transgressions;
he was crushed for our iniquities;
upon him was the chastisement that
brought us peace,
and with his stripes we are healed.
6 All we like sheep have gone astray;
we have turned—every one—to his own
way;
and the LORD has laid on him
the iniquity of us all.

7 He was oppressed, and he was afflicted,
yet he opened not his mouth;
like a lamb that is led to the slaughter,
and like a sheep that before its shearers
is silent,

so he opened not his mouth.
8 By oppression and judgment he was taken
away;
and as for his generation, who
considered
that he was cut off out of the land of the
living,
stricken for the transgression of my
people?
9 And they made his grave with the wicked
and with a rich man in his death,
although he had done no violence,
and there was no deceit in his mouth.

10 Yet it was the will of the LORD to crush
him;
he has put him to grief;
when his soul makes an offering for guilt,
he shall see his offspring; he shall
prolong his days;
the will of the LORD shall prosper in his hand.
11 Out of the anguish of his soul he shall see
and be satisfied;
by his knowledge shall the righteous one,
my servant,
make many to be accounted righteous,
and he shall bear their iniquities.
12 Therefore I will divide him a portion with
the many,
and he shall divide the spoil with the
strong,
because he poured out his soul to death
and was numbered with the
transgressors;
yet he bore the sin of many,
and makes intercession for the
transgressors.

Exodus 7:11-24 (Reading 53)

Then Pharaoh summoned the wise men and the sorcerers, and they, the magicians of Egypt, also did the same by their secret arts. 12 For each man cast down his staff, and they became serpents. But Aaron's staff swallowed up their staffs. 13 Still Pharaoh's heart was hardened, and he would not listen to them, as the Lord had said.

14 Then the Lord said to Moses, "Pharaoh's heart is hardened; he refuses to let the people go. 15 Go to Pharaoh in the morning, as he is going out to the water. Stand on the bank of the Nile to meet him, and take in your hand the staff that turned into a serpent. 16 And you shall say to him, 'The Lord, the God of the Hebrews, sent me to you, saying, "Let my people go, that they may serve me in the wilderness. But so far, you have not obeyed." 17 Thus says the Lord, "By this you shall know that I am the Lord: behold, with the staff that is in my hand I will strike the water that is in the Nile, and it shall turn into blood. 18 The fish in the Nile shall die, and the Nile will stink, and the Egyptians will grow weary of drinking water from the Nile.""" 19 And the Lord said to Moses, "Say to Aaron, 'Take your staff and stretch out your hand over the waters of Egypt, over their rivers, their canals, and their ponds, and all their pools of water, so that they may become blood, and there shall be blood throughout all the land of Egypt, even in vessels of wood and in vessels of stone.'"

20 Moses and Aaron did as the Lord commanded. In the sight of Pharaoh and in the sight of his servants he lifted up the staff and struck the water in the Nile, and all the water in the Nile turned into blood. 21 And the fish in the Nile died, and the Nile stank, so that the Egyptians could not drink water from the Nile. There was blood throughout all the land of Egypt. 22 But the magicians of Egypt did the same by their secret arts. So Pharaoh's heart remained hardened, and he would not listen to them, as the Lord had said. 23 Pharaoh turned and went into his house, and he did not take even this to heart. 24 And all the Egyptians dug along the Nile for water to drink, for they could not drink the water of the Nile.

matthiasmedia

Matthias Media is a ministry team of like-minded, evangelical Christians working together to achieve a particular goal, as summarized in our mission statement:

To serve our Lord Jesus Christ, and the growth of his gospel in the world, by producing and delivering high quality, Bible-based resources.

It was in 1988 that we first started pursuing this mission together, and in God's kindness we now have more than 250 different ministry resources being distributed all over the world. These resources range from Bible studies and books through to training courses and audio sermons.

To find out more about our large range of very useful products, and to access samples and free downloads, visit our website:

www.matthiasmedia.com.au

How to buy our resources

1. Direct from us over the internet:
    – in the US: www.matthiasmedia.com
    – in Australia and the rest of the world: www.matthiasmedia.com.au

2. Direct from us by phone:
    – in the US: 1 866 407 4530
    – in Australia: 1800 814 360 (Sydney: 9663 1478)
    – international: +61-2-9663-1478

3. Through a range of outlets in various parts of the world. Visit **www.matthiasmedia.com.au/international.php** for details about recommended retailers in your part of the world, including www.thegoodbook.co.uk in the United Kingdom.

4. Trade enquiries can be addressed to:
    – in the US: sales@matthiasmedia.com
    – in the UK: sales@ivpbooks.com
    – in Australia and the rest of the world: sales@matthiasmedia.com.au

MORE DAILY READINGS ...

Volume 1
60 readings from Matthew 5-6, Joshua and 1 Corinthians 1-4.

Volume 2
60 readings from 1 Corinthians 5-7, Malachi and topical passages about God's trinitarian characteristics.

Volume 3
55 readings from Genesis 1-11, 2 Thessalonians, Hebrews 1-7 and topical passages about Jesus.

Volume 4
60 readings from Matthew 8-16, Nehemiah and Hebrews 8-13.

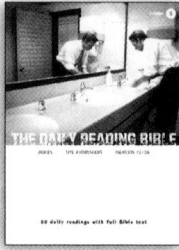
Volume 5
60 readings from James, Genesis 12-35 and topical passages about the atonement.

Volume 6
60 readings from Ephesians, Lamentations and Proverbs.

Volume 7
62 readings from 1 Peter, Zechariah, Revelation 1-3 and topical passages about our present suffering.

Volume 8
60 readings from John 1-12, Hosea and studies on words.

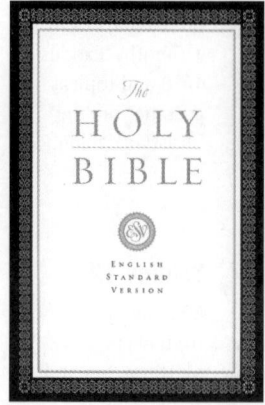